Online Social Networking on Campus

In the era of such online spaces as Facebook, Instant Messenger, Live Journal, Blogger, Web Shots, and campus blogs, college students are using these resources and other online sites as a social medium. Inevitably, this medium presents students with ethical decisions about social propriety, self disclosure and acceptable behaviour. Because online social networking sites have proven problematic for college students and for college administrators, this book aims to offer professional guidance to Higher Education administrators and policy makers.

Online Social Networking on Campus: Understanding What Matters in Student Culture is a professional guide for Higher Education faculty and Student Affairs administrators, which rigorously examines college students' use of online social networking sites and how they use these to develop relationships both on and off campus. Most importantly, *Online Social Networking on Campus* investigates how college students use online sites to explore and make sense of their identities. Providing information taken from interviews, surveys, and focus group data, the book presents an ethnographic view of social networking that will help Student Affairs administrators, Information Technology administrators, and faculty better understand and provide guidance to the "neomillennials" on their campuses.

Ana M. Martínez Alemán is Associate Professor of Education and Chair of the Department of Educational Administration and Higher Education at the Lynch School of Education, Boston College.

Katherine Lynk Wartman is a PhD candidate at Boston College, a resident director at Simmons College in Boston, MA, and has served as Parent and Family Relations and Special Projects Administrator at Colby-Sawyer College.

Online Social Networking on Campus

Understanding What Matters in Student Culture

Ana M. Martínez Alemán

and

Katherine Lynk Wartman

Routledge
Taylor & Francis Group

NEW YORK AND LONDON

First published 2009
by Routledge
270 Madison Ave, New York, NY 10016

Simultaneously published in the UK
by Routledge
2 Park Square, Milton Park, Abingdon, Oxon OX14 4RN

Routledge is an imprint of the Taylor & Francis Group, an informa business

Typeset in Caslon and Trade Gothic by EvS Communication Networx, Inc.
Printed and bound in the United States of America on acid-free paper by Walsworth
Publishing Company, Marceline, MO

Library of Congress Cataloging in Publication Data
Martínez Alemán, Ana M.
Online social networking on campus : understanding what matters in student culture
/ Ana M. Martinez Aleman, [Katherine Lynk Wartman]. — 1st ed.
p. cm.
1. College students—Social networks—United States. 2. Online social networks—
United States. I. Wartman, Katherine Lynk. II. Title.
LA229.M345 2008
302.23'1—dc22
2008027318

ISBN 10: 0-415-99019-X (hbk)
ISBN 10: 0-415-99020-3 (pbk)
ISBN 10: 0-203-88496-5 (ebk)

ISBN 13: 978-0-415-99019-6 (hbk)
ISBN 13: 978-0-415-99020-2 (pbk)
ISBN 13: 978-0-203-88496-6 (ebk)

Contents

Preface

Any technological advancement presents social scientists with an opportunity to gain insight into human behavior, and the innovation of online social networking has presented those of us interested in understanding college and university cultures with an especially rich one. We embarked on this project eager to know how this early 21st century generation of college and university students appreciate, value, construct, and negotiate student culture online. A project that required us to be transgenerational ethnographers, this examination tested our ability to interpret the meaning that students make of this new cultural space, all the while recognizing the difficulties and risks that are inherent in the translation of meaning across generations, across conceptual paradigms. In this project, then, we were generational strangers kindly and often enthusiastically welcomed into college and university students' online social worlds. In this book, we endeavor to translate online college culture, but we take care to avoid the appropriation of students' voices. In what Paul Ricoeur (2004) would characterize as "linguistic hospitality," to this end, this book is our best translation of online college culture in which students speak for themselves, and we as researchers transport them—the authors of the meaning of online campus culture—to the reader.

In the chapters that follow, we hope to provide insight into the dynamic that computer-mediated communication (CMC) through online social network sites (SNS) has brought to college campus culture and in doing so will help both student affairs practitioners and higher education researchers better understand contemporary online college culture. We have passed the point where the online social communities of college students can be considered "Their Space." To these students, the communities are real, extending from and intertwining with their day-to-day lives on traditional college campuses. The new campus includes the online campus. Understanding how students' make use of Facebook has implications for specific administrative areas of college campuses such as judicial affairs, college counseling, new student orientation, first-year experience programs, student leadership, residence life, campus activities, career development, athletics, Greek life, information technology, and admissions. These offices should certainly be aware of potentially negative effects of Facebook, but also how these sites are and can be used creatively and productively to benefit students' development and to build positive campus communities.

Specifically in this text, we will explore with students the role Facebook plays in the construction of gender and ethnic identity on campus, and how this online platform influences the construction of group identity for campus organizations through the ethnographic presentation of diverse students from different campuses. Through holistic examination that is highlighted by synchronous ethnographic tours of student online profiles, we have asked students to describe and examine the role Facebook plays in their campus cultures, their perception of the value of their Facebook use, and to explain and interpret behavior on these sites. This college generation has moved from asynchronous e-mail communication to instant messaging; they send text messages on cell phones, subscribe and contribute to online blogs and journals, and post photographs of themselves online. And yet we know very little about their use of online social networks. We invited students to talk about their use—how and why they use Facebook, what they believe to be its rewards and its problems, what effects they perceive it to have on campus culture. In what follows, we present the views of student online social networking enriched by the voices of students—the insiders' view of the digital phenomenon. We present an ethnographic vista of the value of social networking sites as portrayed by a diversity of residential undergraduate students enrolled at a variety of colleges and universities in the United States, including all of the original institutions to have Facebook. Some students you'll hear from currently attend coeducational institutions; others are enrolled in single-sex colleges. Some students are the first in their family to attend college, while others are continuing a family legacy of college or university enrollment. Some students are racial or ethnic minorities on their campuses; some students self-identify as gay and lesbian.

In chapter 2, "Emergence and Acceleration: Computer-Mediated Communication and the College Student," we chronicle the development and rise of online social networks. This chapter presents an overview of the development of these sites and their popularization among the current generation of college students. We will explore the broader, cultural phenomenon of the Internet in the context of college student use and examine the contemporary landscape of digital media used by college students today. In chapter 3, we address college student use of online social networking sites as it is reflected in data collected in a multimethod study. First, we will present a primer of the functions of Facebook so that someone not intimately familiar with this online social network site can gain an understanding of how it operates. Overall, this chapter will present the student's perspective— how and why students use these sites—as revealed in the research data. What will emerge in this chapter is a picture of the centrality of online networking sites in contemporary campus life and how these sites are perceived as an expansion of the "bricks and mortar" campus.

In this third chapter, "Students Speak: Campus Culture, Identity, and Facebook," the spotlight is on the voices of representative students. We present students across a spectrum of identities important to the consideration of campus culture, identities informed by race or ethnicity, gender and sexuality, and socioeconomic class. We present students' views or the meaning they make of online behaviors and discuss how social networking sites have impacted these individual students, but also what effects social networking may be having on the college campus culture. We asked these students to reflect on the role Facebook has played in the overall development of the college community—in such areas as residence halls, athletic teams, or between students. We asked them to consider how Facebook, through their presentation of a myriad of visual images, can perpetuate standards of behavior in a college or university community and create social norms.

In the penultimate chapter, "The New Campus Reality: Facebook and Student Affairs Practice," we present frameworks for understanding Facebook. How can college student affairs professionals seize the productive power of these sites and utilize them to engender positive campus community? And given the developmental velocity and sophistication of its applications, how does the college student affairs professional respond to and keep pace with Facebook use? What should college and university administrators know about Facebook so that they can take appropriate action on student and parent demands? To conclude, we ponder "The Future of the Campus Social Graph" in chapter 5. How will the changing demographics of online social network users affect college student use and the cultural norms built within the walled community of Facebook? What is on the horizon for online campus culture?

Today the online world of social networking dominates the real college and university campus. What does this mean to students and what are we—as parents, faculty, and administrators—to understand from their estimation? In the pages that follow, we consider these and other questions.

We thank Boston College and the Lynch School of Education for the funding that enabled us to explore and probe the nature of online campus culture. Most importantly, we are grateful to the students who shared with us their appreciation for, misgivings about, and generational perspectives on Facebook and online campus culture. This book would have been impossible without them. The encouragement and support of our families, friends, and colleagues throughout this project was invaluable.

1

INTRODUCTION

Campus Life Online

I don't often walk around with words printed on my body about my interests…but Facebook is just an extension of me. I try to put my personality on the page, which is difficult because it is a set format. But through photos of myself and the way I word things, I can present my personality in my page.

—Laura, undergraduate Facebook member

Unlike the generations of college students that predated the inception of the World Wide Web, the college student today experiences college in both real and virtual communities. Early adapters of Internet technology, today's college students are active in several online communities in which they explore new forms of self-expression, create connections in the past improbable, and more and more blur the line between their real worlds and their virtual worlds. As high school students they grew up in a generation of computer-mediated communication media that had already moved beyond basic mailing lists and LISTSERVs. Their adolescent years are characterized by their use of Instant Messenger and MySpace, the interactive social networking website most popular among high school students. They joined virtual communities such as Friendster and visited photo sharing websites such as Webshots. By the time they reached college, 88% were using the Internet daily and 86% brought their own computers to college (Studentmonitor.com, 2008).

The generation of students attending college and universities today was born into a world in which technology was a well-established and rapidly intensifying part of everyday life. The personal computer, named "Machine of the Year" by *Time Magazine* in 1982, was already an element of businesses, schools, and homes by the late 1980s. By the time today's college students were in elementary school in the mid- to late 1990s, the World Wide Web was already up and running, over 50 million people worldwide were cellular phone users, and early social networking sites (e.g., SixDegrees.com and LiveJournal.com) were part of the technological landscape. By the time they reached secondary school, today's college and university students had experienced the online worlds of Wikipedia, uploaded photos to Flickr, perhaps purchased recorded music in a CD format or simply downloaded music from Napster, or moved to the portable media player introduced by Apple in 2001, the iPod, to more efficiently customize their music play lists in a convenient form. By the time they enrolled in college, our students were likely to have had experience with MySpace, YouTube, podcasts, Bebo, and Facebook. For some, their computer-mediated communications now include a wireless, handheld, Internet-enabled, multimedia iPhone (released November 2007).

What role does computer-mediated communication play in the lives of college students? Most especially, what function do social networking sites serve for college students and what meanings do students make of these media? College administrators, parents, and researchers know little about how and why college students develop online social networks. There has not been a serious ethnographic exploration of the role that virtual communities play in college student life. We really do not have a rich view of how college students use these sights productively, or how these sites help construct college cultures today. We have not heard the voices of college students as they describe, explain, and interpret the value of social networking sites for their own college experience. Typically, students' accounts of the role of social networking sites in the growth and maintenance of college and university cultures and communities are quick sound bites in popular media. We are interested in presenting diverse voices of college and university students to elucidate the multiple meanings of computer-mediated social networking on campuses.

We most often hear about the problems associated with social networking sites. Journalists report on misuse that ranges from students in the United Kingdom surfing social networking sites during class to more serious concerns about capturing and instantly disseminating dangerous or offensive student behavior (whether posed or actual). Party photos of Olympic swimmer and world record holder Australian Stephanie Rice consuming alcohol were posted and immediately viewed by Facebook users and made public in the press. Photos of inebriated young women and men are often showcased on these sites, raising concerns among college administrators and alcohol counselors about binge-drinking behavior and the consequences of the accessibility of these photos by future employers. In the United States, scholarship athletes' behavior is often scrutinized on sites like Facebook, the second most-trafficked social networking site in the world (ComScore, 2007; Schonfeld, 2007).

Though residential and student life administrators on college campuses have begun to use social networking sites to check student comportment, many now look to these sites to help students and to facilitate their transitions to and in college. San Francisco State University housing officials now ask incoming first-year students to review online the profiles of other new students in order to make better roommate matches and perhaps avoid problems and complaints down the road. Many U.S. high school seniors now scan Facebook profiles for students who will be attending their chosen college or university. During their precollege summer these students begin to use social networking sites as a precursor to campus orientation activities designed to integrate students socially. Once on campus, they harness the power of social network sites to advance and promote campus activities. Fraternities and sororities, student governments, and campus student activities groups now use social networking sites like Facebook to invite students to their events, to post important announcements, and to carry on the day-to-day business of the group. Students also network on sites for social, environmental, and honorable causes, for political candidates, and for philanthropies and charity fund-raising events. Social network sites are often used by students to create communal feelings among dormitory or residence hall mates, racial and ethnic minority students, and gay and lesbian students. Part campus bulletin board and part campus square, social networking sites are now fundamental to the culture of the campus and student life. And even faculty, who are often ambivalent about their own participation in social networking sites used by students, and whose participation is considered problematic by students, recognize that they can reconnect with favorite former students and be kept informed of alumni accomplishments. These sites also provide a communication avenue for particular seminars or as in the case of fine arts faculty, announce auditions, performances, and exhibitions to current students. Some faculty charged with first year advisories or tutorials find social networking sites useful to communicate and become acquainted with new students over the summer preceding the start of college in the fall.

It is now unmistakable that in the era of online social spaces like Facebook, Instant Messenger (IM), Live Journal, Xanga, Web Shots, Blogger.com, and Bebo college students use these and other online sites as a social medium, a space where they explore their identities, where they produce and reproduce rules for behavior, where they make public self-representations through text and images. Students use these sites to interact and bond with other students, to share experiences, and to participate in the new online college "community" that is understood by students to be real. Through the myriad of social networking functions that currently exist and advance at a hurried pace, college students communicate personal information, share photographs of themselves and others, extend invitations to social events, and reconnect with high school and childhood friends. Inevitably, each of these functions and their representations presents students with ethical decisions about social propriety, self-disclosure, and acceptable behavior.

Worldwide, social networking sites are an established trend. Sites like Friendster, Orkut, Mixi, LunarStorm, and Bebo are commonly used across Europe, Latin America, and the Pacific. The U.S.-launched Facebook reports that 14.5% of its users are in Canada and 11.6% in the United Kingdom. In China, Xiaonei has become the most popular Internet site. Started in December 2005 by Tsinghua University graduates, Xiaonei targets and restricts its use to college students. Founded in 2002, hi5 is the most popular social networking site in Central American countries such as Costa Rica, Ecuador, Guatemala, and Nicaragua. In Mexico, hi5 is the fifth most visited Internet site behind Google, Windows Live, YouTube, and Metroflog.

The social network for high school and college students, Bebo, is the seventh most popular Internet site in New Zealand, followed closely by Facebook. In France the second most popular website is the social networking site, Skyrock, also the sixth most popular site in Senegal; it is equally popular in the Indian Ocean island-nation of the Republic of Madagascar. In Pakistan, the social networking site Orkut is the fourth most visited website. Facebook, holding the fifth spot in the top sites visited in the United States, finds itself in the top 10 of the most visited sites in countries like Turkey (no. 2), Sudan (no. 6), the United Kingdom (no. 2), Bahrain (no. 6), and South Africa (no. 2) (Alexa.com, 2007). As a global phenomenon, social networking through computer-mediated communication, whether through Facebook or other sites, is an established trend (Alexa.com, 2007).

Not coincidentally, given the swift rise and evident ubiquity of social networking sites among the college and university-going population worldwide, scholars' and researchers' interest in virtual communities is reasonably new. Among social scientists, interest in computer-mediated communication and social networking sites is typically focused on the sociology and psychology of student relationships, self-esteem, and engagement with college. Some researchers have established a positive relationship between Facebook use and a student's formation and maintenance of social capital; that is, a student's ability to stay connected with a community (Ellison, Steinfield, & Lampe, 2007). Others have revealed unequal participation based on gender, race and ethnicity, and parental educational level in social networking sites such as Facebook, MySpace, Xanga, and Friendster (Hargittai, 2007). Communications researchers now concern themselves with how virtual communication affects behavior. For example, the Stanford University Virtual Human Interaction Laboratory has supported research that suggests that online social behavior can change real life behavior (Bailenson, Yee, Blascovich, & Guadagno, 2008), insinuating that positive social actions and deeds established online can be transferred to our daily lives. Ethics scholars and analysts of public policy have also tried to make sense of the moral issues raised by social networking, some stipulating that these sites reflect a "new narcissism" (Rosen, 2007) and that the related phenomenon of the "privacy paradox" that social networking sites have produced (Barnes, 2006) requires principled consideration. In surveys conducted between 1995 and 2000, researchers Katz and Rice tried to document the synergy between Americans' online lives and their real lives and noted the use of the Internet and user identity. They argue that as "public diaries" Facebook and MySpace function as panopticons in which behavior is shaped or manipulated simply because it is being "seen" by others, or more to the point, that private behavior has become public action (Katz & Rice, 2002).

National research endeavors have also been newly inaugurated. Extensive and broad assessments of social networking sites' use and their likely positive effects on users have been conducted by governmental agencies such as the United Kingdom's Office of Communications in their report, "Social Networking: A Quantitative and Qualitative Research Report into Attitudes, Behaviors and Use" (2008). Noting that social networking sites like MySpace, Bebo, and Facebook are now "a mainstream communication technology for many people" (Executive Summary), the report captures the popularity and generational differences among users and constructs a typology of users.

In the United States, the Pew Charitable Trusts and Research Center has supported the Internet and American Life Project that has collected data on the impact of technology and the Internet on Americans. In their most recent study, "Teens and Social Media: The Use of Social Media Gains a Greater Foothold in Teen Life as They Embrace the Conversational Nature of Interactive Online Media" (Lenhart, Madden, Rankin, & Smith, 2007), Pew researchers explain that for teens social networking sites help them manage friendships; that is, teenagers use these sites to make plans with their friends, to stay in touch with friends that they don't often see, and to make new friends. The Pew reports that for a small minority of teenagers, social networking sites are used as a platform on which to flirt with others. Overwhelmingly, young women and men who are MySpace users in high school, migrate to Facebook once in college. In a recent University of Michigan study, for example, 99.5% of all students at the university had Facebook profiles and reported that as is the case with high school use, college students use the site to communicate with existing friends (Matney, Borland, & Cope, 2008). Now known as "the Facebook Generation" (Bugeja, 2006), today's college students engage in online social life primarily on Facebook

Given the overwhelming popularity of Facebook among college and university students, it is important to gain an understanding of the meaning and importance that college and university students give this particular social networking site. What is the student perspective on Facebook? How have students integrated this site into their everyday lives on campus? What value do they give to Facebook and its functions? What norms of campus culture have been instituted by Facebook use and how do students react to these norms? These are the central questions we aim to address in this book.

The use of online social networking sites (SNS) is dominant in contemporary culture, but what makes Facebook so relevant to campus culture? Facebook is the most frequently visited site on college campuses and the fifth most trafficked site on the Internet overall. It is reported that over 85% of all college and university students use Facebook (Arrington, 2005). In the study described in this book, the average amount of time students said they spent on Facebook per week was 6.2 hours, while the number of times per day they said that they logged into the site was 6.3 times. Globally, the average minutes spent on Facebook by visitors to the site averaged 186 each day, and over 26.6 million visited the site just in May 2007. Almost half of all users return to the site each day, and on average will spend 25 minutes on the site daily (ComScore, 2007). Though a growing number of noncollege students now use the site, college students still make up the largest percentage of Facebook users (Insidefacebook.com). In 2008, Facebook was surpassed only by Google, Yahoo!, MySpace and YouTube in site popularity in the United States (Alexa.com, 2008).

Prior to the development of Facebook in February 2004, when college students communicated with each other online they did so through text messaging. Designed especially for this "niche community," Facebook brought to college campuses an online, virtual version of the historic paper facebook complete with photographs (boyd & Ellison, 2007). The original paper facebook distributed on campuses every fall to incoming first year students served as a directory for the campus and included photographs of students and administrators. The new virtual Facebook does that and more. Facebook now serves as the primary social networking site on campuses. Through Facebook students connect, meet, exchange information, extend invitations to events and parties, form interest groups, and view and exchange photos and videos. In effect, Facebook as a social networking site emulates offline relationships common to the college campus. As a means to get to know other students, or stay in contact with friends on other college campuses worldwide, Facebook exponentially expands college students' "social graph," the map of all of their friends and how all of those friends are connected to each other. College students can now make connections and connect others which in the past was unlikely or at minimum, not as immediate or speedy. These connections are most often already a part of their actual social network but through Facebook, they manage and regulate their social networks, expanding or contracting them through playful caprice or as a serious, reasoned undertaking.

Facebook allows students to join their home college network or any other network (e.g., high school, home town) and move easily on the site through basic navigation. Now the most popular website for uploading photos (14 million photos uploaded daily), Facebook initially restricted use to college students with college or university e-mail addresses. Begun at Harvard University and then first extended to Stanford, Columbia, and Yale Universities, Facebook was made available to Boston, Massachusetts area institutions (Northeastern University, Massachusetts Institute of Technology, Boston University, and Boston College) and other Ivy League schools within two months of its initial launching. Funded through investment capital, Facebook expanded its networks to over 2,000 colleges and universities and 25,000 high schools in the United States, the United Kingdom, and Canada by the end of 2005. Along with its domestic growth in those three countries through 2005, Facebook experienced international growth as well. Now Facebook has high volume active use in Turkey, Australia, France, Sweden, Norway, Colombia, and South Africa (Alexa.com, 2007). In early 2008, Facebook released the site in Spanish and in German (Facebook Press Release, 2008a).

Facebook's reported market appeal is its ability to allow users to digitally map their real world friendships and associations with and through multimedia, while still having control of their privacy online. Protection against identity theft and unwanted dissemination of personal information is a central concern of online users and Facebook provides them with many opportunities to control the distribution of private information. Certified by the independent, privacy information protection service, TRUSTe.org, Facebook users have the power to determine how much information is shared within and across networks, as well as with whom. A site dedicated to giving users direct control over their information, Facebook users have the power to allow or forbid access to their profiles' information to "friends" (other users) they have "confirmed." Users can change privacy settings whenever they choose and have relative autonomy over how much information will constitute their profiles. Users can hide their entire profiles or specific parts of their profiles from all members of a network or groups of friends. Profiles can be "blocked" from view or from access by specific individuals. Facebook also offers users the option of creating a "limited profile" where only pieces of one's full profile are accessible to specified Facebook members. Users can also remove their names from Facebook's search feature for members, as well as remove their names from nonmember search engines like Google or Yahoo! (Vander Veer, 2008).

In addition to the privacy settings for individual users, college and university students find on Facebook many features that mimic the real-life campus as well as expand an individual's reach within and across campuses. Facebook's "Wall" is the space on individual user profiles where text messages can be posted or uploaded as attachments; an unlimited number of photographs and videos can be uploaded into "Albums"; "Pokes" are used to prod or nudge another user to communicate. The "News Feed" is a rundown of friends' recent activities, changes in their status, or approaching events. Virtual gifts can be sent to friends on Facebook through the "Gifts" application, and in the "Marketplace" users can post ads to buy or sell items. In total, there are over 24,000 "applications" that users can employ on their profiles, applications ranging from political bumper stickers to music preferences to career and employment groupings. Facebook users can post and invite other users to "open" or "closed" real world events, and can also search or browse for events. Facebook can also be accessed on the user's Internet enabled mobile phone or other wireless handheld devices through the "Facebook Mobile" feature.

Facebook is a milestone in the 21st century college experience, especially in the social and extracurricular experiences of undergraduates. The campus "social" is now also online. But as with other technological developments, online social networking sites such as Facebook have proven problematic for college students and for college administrators. The posting of compromising photographs on such sites as Facebook has injected the real world of campus judicial affairs into students' virtual worlds. Text messaging forums have become vehicles for student-to-student harassment, and employers have begun to use social network sites to check the integrity of student applicants. Oversight and management of student use of these sites has become a central concern of campus administrators and college legal counsel. Student affairs administrators are struggling to understand students' Facebook use and its potential impact on the users' personal development. These administrators share a concern about students' self-expression in this forum, particularly about the public showcase of images that display problematic behavior. Often professionally ambivalent about their status as being in loco parentis, student affairs administrators do question whether they should monitor the conduct in these online venues (Read & Young, 2006).

2

EMERGENCE AND ACCELERATION

Computer-Mediated Communication and the College Student

As new media grows in connectivity, content, applications, and user populations, a new kind of transparency is emerging. Increasingly, Net-geners don't see the technology at all. They see people, information, games, applications, services, friends and protagonists at the other end. They don't see a computer screen.

—Tapscott, 1998, p. 39

The Rise of the Technological Generation and the Construction of Individual Identity and College Culture

It can be argued that late 20th-century cultural shifts in the salience of identity were fertile ground or minimally a timely occurrence for the development of computer-mediated communication and especially so for the growth of online social networking sites. Worldwide we experienced many contestations to historic constructions of social identity in the late 20th century. In the last half of the century, the politics of nationality, race, gender, sexuality, and hegemonic power were challenged by ideological rebellion in economic, social, and political spheres. Colonial power was challenged and in most cases defeated. The articulation of global economic disparities was mainstreamed. Opposition to racial and ethnic inequality and oppression, whether it was de jure or de facto, was widespread across nations. Motivated by an antagonism to the normative claims of Western societies, a postmodern and critical theorizing and political activity took hold in many societies uncovering and disclosing identity and cultural possibilities that could define who we "are" as individual social beings, and who we "are" as members of groups.

In the United States, especially, the challenge to modernism's identity norms in the latter decades of the 20th century by feminism, critical racial and ethnic movements, and discourses on sexuality informed a consciousness about the politics of identity—the experiences that shaped who one "was"—that mattered greatly in our social worlds and that social standard-bearers such as "masculinity," "heterosexuality," "Whiteness," were an ill fit for most of the population. In Western Europe, the critique of a fixed, normative construction of identity was framed by an accounting of historic colonial oppression. Delivered through postcolonial appraisal, a new consciousness of individual and cultural identity emerged that stipulated that the historic and experiential factors of colonialism marked the cultural identity of those colonized by other societies. Self-definition in this sense allows for individual identity to be informed by both unique and collective experiences, and for collective identity to be shaped by colonial history and the experiences of subjugated groups. The analysis of oppression and presumed inferiority of social groups was the centerpiece of this cultural critique.

In the late 20th century, these political and intellectual claims had some bearing on campus cultures, fueled in large part by academic discourses and research critical of normative claims on individual and group identity. The college campus, especially in the United States, became the hotbed of "identity politics," a logical community for cultural dispute, inquiry, and wrangling. Through academic theorizing, discourse, and empirical research, identity and its relationship to culture was dissected and reorganized on campus by the faculty. Their students, developmentally predisposed to the relevance of identity, were the perfect observers and participants in the reconstitution of our understanding of individual and group identity by the close of the century. The conviction that life experience and not "universal" principles should craft politics and education was foremost in the attitudes around identity.

Campus culture in the 1990s in the United States reflected broader social concerns and unease over the traditional hegemony of Western, modernist ideas about self and the authority given its knowledge claims. Fueled and grounded in the campus political rebellion and reforms of the 1960s, the culture wars on America's campuses 30 years later were their ideological progeny. Informed by both the broader social misgivings over historic hegemonic forces and their parents' generational politics, college student consciousness was confronted by scholars and researchers who had begun to challenge the ethnocentrism of the liberal arts curriculum, and especially in the humanities and philosophy, had destabilized disciplinary values. Postmodern and feminist critiques in the humanities and social sciences brought to students a reconsideration of sexuality, gender roles, racial and ethnic identity, and the historic contexts in which they were framed. On campus, multicultural pluralism and its implications for individual and group distinctiveness, was tacitly understood as achievable in a liberal democracy.

On campus, the politics of identity took the form of curricular revision to include new critical scholarship and research, demands for transparency in administrative practices, and for a more authentic institutional actuation of social justice or equity agenda. Affirmative action in admissions was a flash point for these considerations on college and university campuses, as were abortion rights and gender equity, the underrepresentation of racial and ethnic groups within the ranks of the faculty, and the characterization of pornography. American colleges and universities in the last decade of the 20th century were cultures in which the politics of difference—those historic constructs that created and reinforced race, gender, and class privilege—were the epistemological and metaphysical salvos common on campus. Young academic scholars questioned the veracity of universal constructions of self and identity. Students demanded curricular change to include the historically marginalized experiences of women, racial and ethnic groups, and gays and lesbians. The ethnocentric curriculum was viewed as the primary means for social reproduction and the newly self-conscious student and faculty challenged these claims by communicating counter-normative experiences. The shared experiences of injustice, whether political, economic, or societal by individuals as an outcome of group membership, were claimed as epistemologically relevant by students and faculty, pitting them against mainstream curricular objectives. Despite Arthur Schlesinger's (1992) warning that the politics of difference would undermine civil liberty, the belief in and value of a "common" culture and set of ideas was resisted on many college and university campuses. Instead, the transformation of identity could be achieved through the expansion of consciousness through a reconceived, reconfigured curriculum. Thus, by the last decade of the century when personal computing and the Internet were rapidly becoming ubiquitous conventions, how individual and cultural identity were conceived and realized through student activities and identity-specific clubs and organizations was cultural work done on campus and that informed and cultivated campus culture.

Internet History and Use

Concurrent with the broad social movements that shaped the culture of campus life in the late 20th century, technological developments in the 1970s through the 1990s empowered individual users to communicate in ways never before experienced. In the late 1960s communication mediated by computers was largely the province of scientists in research centers and universities. Computer-mediated communication was conducted between a computer and localized networks or mainframes, and there was no synchronized system through which all computers could be unified, ostensibly enabling random and global computer-to-computer communication across networks. Connecting separate systems of computer-mediated communication required some form of technical innovation or breakthrough that would unify different network protocols; that is, translate the rules or protocols that enable data to be communicated between computer terminals. Protocols governed the syntax, semantics, and coordination of data transfers between networks, and thus communication between networks—internetwork communication—was cumbersome, restricted to the few sites that could manage large amounts of data, or was just impossible.

It would not be until 1969 in the ARPANET project when "packet switching," the protocol that could translate or connect separate systems was effectively developed. Previously explored in the early 1960s this technique could send and receive data quickly and efficiently across local and long distance connections. The technical linguistic friendliness of packet switching enabled the subsequent unification of all network protocols, and in 1974, the "Internetwork protocol" (IP) was launched. Joining any network or series of networks together, the IP could utilize any system's infrastructure. Faster and cheaper than maintaining isolated or dedicated networks, the IP could also transfer data simultaneously. Thus, what had begun as an era in which data were laboriously transferred from machine to machine within a specified network, evolved to make possible global and large scale networking by individual, nonexpert users. The eventual commercialization of the IP would not occur in earnest until the development of user-friendly, multimedia enabled computing in the late 1980s and its innovations through the decade of the 1990s.

As a result, user-friendly computing was not an essential condition of the American college campus until the 1990s. Direct operation of computers by individual college and university students did not come about in earnest until the mass-marketing of Apple's Lisa personal computer in the early 1980s. The personal home computer marketed by IBM a few years earlier did not have the graphical user interface (GUI) that the Apple Lisa could deliver to nonresearcher, nonexpert users, and by the mid-1980s the Macintosh personal computer displaced Apple's Lisa with its easier, mouse-driven GUIs and mass-market appeal. Innovations continued through the decade with increased momentum so that by the late 1990s, the era when the Internet became a reality, individual, nonexpert, user-friendly computing included easy plug and play devices for digital and video cameras, and increasingly more sophisticated peripherals like laser printers and scanners. With the development and implementation of hypertext in the late 1980s, college students could interface through text with other related information. With hypertext, students could gather information through hyperlinks, or connections to associated data, and actively look at and communicate information. By the early 21st century, personal computers are more mobile with the successful production of portable laptops and capability for wireless communication between these and other personal computers is possible through preinstalled wireless capability. Thus, by the time college students entered college in the early years of the century, they were knowledgeable and competent users of convenient, highly efficient, and media-rich computing. In fact, they entered college or universities already experienced in the culture of personal computing, and as students, took for granted that technology is their way of life.

Central to the advancement of personal computing and pivotal to user-friendly computer-mediated communication on college and university campuses were the improvements and enhancements to operating systems that could enable the quick, uncomplicated, straightforward operation that is necessary for online social networking sites like Facebook. Already able to interact with their personal computers and peripheral devices, college culture did not truly experience the impact of computer-mediated communication between students until 1985 when Microsoft introduced its Windows operating system. With the advent of Windows personal computing truly became user-friendly and changed the landscape of personal computer-mediated communication. Equipped with greater multimedia capabilities, Windows and its subsequent generations, such as Windows 3.0, Windows 95, Windows XP, and Vista in 2007, captured the personal computer market with its easy, straightforward graphical user interface (GUI). Before Microsoft Windows, computer users had to either type commands or follow complex text menus to run software. Windows brought to the noncomputing expert, sets of images or icons that served as visual pointers to instruct the software. A user's manipulation of the icons enabled the nonexpert to efficiently and properly instruct the computer to engage in a variety of processes. Windows gave individual college student-users greater access to and facility with multimedia, ushering in the era in which students not only consumed knowledge through technology but produced it as well. College students had been a target market for Apple's Macintosh since 1985 and when in 1997 Apple partnered with Microsoft to equip Macs with Windows, college students experienced computing like never before. Targeted to colleges and universities, public schools and home users, Apple's Macintosh with Windows capabilities was advertised and sold with popular culture in mind. Aesthetics and user-friendly capabilities were pitched at the younger user. In the ensuing years (1998–2001), college students would be primary consumers of iMac and iBook, all Apple hardware with immensely improved speed and graphical capability, but more importantly, easy Internet access (Levy, 1994). The "i" before these products signaled to consumers that the rapidly expanding Internet was a mouse click away. As advertised, the iMac was meant to meet the consumer's "excitement of the Internet" with "the simplicity of the Macintosh." In other words, the era of fast, high quality, user-friendly, and aesthetically pleasing personal computing had arrived. But more to the point, iMac reflected the industry's realization that technology was situated centrally within popular culture, especially youth culture. Consumers, and specifically its younger demographic, were keenly interested in simple, fast, and sophisticated computing as a gateway to the ever-expanding range of possibilities of the Internet. Culture and commerce had been invaded, shaped, and produced by the Internet in the late 20th century, a time when 20% of college students reported having used computers between the ages of 5 and 8, 100% had used computers by the time they were 16 to 18 years old, and 50% had begun using the Internet before attending college (Jones, 2002).

By the early 1990s students could actively "browse" the newly con-stituted Internet. Unlocking the then embryonic Internet, the user interface Mosaic enabled the embedding of images in text rather than in a separate window, allowing for a more efficient navigation. Compatible with Windows and graphically seductive, Mosaic was integral in setting the foundation for the explosion of Internet use in the 1990s (Reid, 1997). Other browsers like Netscape would take hold on the early 1990s, soon followed by Internet Explorer, Firefox, Camino, and others. By 2001, when Google had already established itself as the premier Internet search engine, students could retrieve text and graphic data instantaneously and with little effort. Individual students could very easily seek out or search for targeted information, whether text, graphic, or audio. Information embedded in multimedia could be produced, shared, transmitted, and consumed by students at accelerated speeds. Already able to share music files through Napster, by 2003 commercial vendors had set up shop on the Internet to sell music downloaded as digital files to individual computers. A central element of late adolescent development, purchasing or owning music was a logical locus of college student Internet use. By 2008, online music stores like iTunes cornered the music-buying market over real, brick and mortar retailer Wal-Mart. This was the first time online, digital music consumption has bettered the purchasing of physical music formats (Quinn & Chmielewski, 2008). Today, some colleges and universities have subscription services with online music stores like Napster to deliver free file-sharing music downloads to their students, but find that most students still prefer to pay-to-own at the virtual store, iTunes (Regan, 2005).

Development of Online Social Networking Sites

Beginning in the 1990s, college and university campuses were sites of high volume use of the Internet. Since 2002, college students, one of the earliest demographic groups to have extensive access to the Internet, are more likely than the general population to go online for fun, to download music, to use chat rooms and e-mail to communicate with friends, parents, and faculty (Jones, 2002). By 2007, three quarters of all college and university students in the United States own a laptop and an iPod. They spend an average of 18 hours every week online, most likely downloading music or communicating through Instant Messenger or social network sites. Undergraduates overwhelmingly (99.9%) believe that the primary purpose of technology is communication, and 81.6% communicate with friends, classmates, and others on social networking sites. According to recent data, students using social networking sites like Facebook mainly reside on a college or university campus (Salaway, Katz, Caruso, Kvavik, & Nelson, 2007).

The ability to publicly identify one's social network through user profiles, and to publicly communicate information about friends in your network—also precursors to the allure of Facebook—were first launched by Friendster, an online dating service founded on the idea that a connection to friends was a valuable recommendation for a potential date (boyd, 2004). Allowing four points or associations of separation from the original friend, Friendster users often browse for fun, to view the profiles of known friends, past and present, "pester" other friends until they respond, and use connections to familiarize themselves with loose acquaintances. As boyd (2004) notes in her ethnographic study of Friendster,

When Milgram coined the term "Familiar Strangers," he was refer-
ring to the strangers that one sees regularly, but never connects with.
Given additional contexts, an individual is quite likely to approach a
familiar stranger. For many, *Friendster* provides that additional context.
In browsing the site, users find people that they often see out. From the
Profile, one can guess another's dating status and sexuality as well as
interests and connections. Often, this is enough additional information
to prompt a user into messaging someone on *Friendster* or approaching
that person offline. (p. 3, ¶ 9)

As a "trust-based or "friendship-based" site (boyd & Ellison, 2007),
Friendster users assumed some safety and control over their online
associations. Friendster "friends" had been vetted by their connections
to other known friends, sometimes close and sometimes acquaintances
within a given social context. The identification with and knowledge
of the social context of the connection seemed to provide users with
some level of security (boyd, 2004). The year following the Friendster
launch, many of the capabilities key to the Friendster site—profiles,
identified networks, and its uses—"pestering," "hooking up," and
identifying "familiar strangers" (boyd, 2004) would appear in Facebook redesigned, reconfigured, and reshaped to fit the college student
audience. Profiles and friends will remain key properties of the site.
The college or university attended will become the network; pestering others to communicate with you becomes "poking"; and users will
trust and give value to the connections of those who contact them or
whom they themselves wish to "friend."

Social Networking Sites as Cultural Phenomenon: In General and on Campus

It is unmistakable that social networking sites have achieved cultural
relevance worldwide. Facebook and MySpace attract over two thirds
of North American Internet users 15 years and older, and Bebo, hi5,
Orkut, and Friendster have strong market shares in other regions
around the globe (ComScore, 2007). According to market analysts,
an essential feature of the regional success of these sites worldwide
is their social or communal importance, at least in the sense that as

commercial entities they have met specific demands of the intended population. Determining a community's consumer desires, social networking sites discern the current consumer needs and anticipate future needs of target populations. Like all forms of computer mediated communication, social networking sites are simultaneously a "medium and an engine of social relations" in which community associations occur and are ordered in some way, and in which the distinctions between what information is private and what information is public is imprecise (Jones, 1998, p. 11). More importantly, these are sites in which individual users and groups create, observe, and interpret culture and in which "the ritual of sharing information pulls it together" (p. 15). Produced by users, the new cultural meanings and values that emerge on these sites evolve from the existing real-world knowledge, commonly held beliefs and customs of a community which at first glance appears distanced from the physical world. On these sites, information sharing rituals and symbolic interactions are cultivated, creating a "second kind of community" (Jones, 1995, p. 20).

As a distinctive sociocultural niche, college campus communities are bound by geography and group membership. This is especially true of residential college campuses in which students live in "socially produced space" constructed by shared knowledge and information, and community beliefs and practices. The social geography of the college campus is reproduced through computer-mediated communication making the online campus "socially produced space" extracted from off-line interactions (Jones, 1995). As a network bounded by group affiliation (being a college student, as well as being a college student at this particular campus), a social network site like Facebook is "tied to offline interactions in a way few other online communities are" (Lampe, Ellison, & Steinfield, 2007, p. 9). Appealing to the niche that is the residential campus, Facebook, like all other online niche communities, must support distinct community cultures, and simultaneously appeal to individual identity needs. In the case of Facebook, the target niche is not homogeneous but is developmentally distinctive, and is both about the individual and the communal. Thus, combining the understanding of the sociology of campus culture as well as the developmental psychology of student users positions Facebook is an online social network that is organized around an identifiable and bounded community that can share interests and social norms, but is simultaneously "egocentric" (boyd & Ellison, 2007). Facebook is a "walled garden" online community.

In the case of Facebook, the network's founders have clearly identified significant elements of the culture of the college community, especially the residential campus, emphasizing the exchange of information within a social network (the college) and across related communities (other colleges). Asserting that its function as a social network is to serve as "a directory grounded in real life," Facebook understands that among college students the exchange of culturally significant information is important. Facebook's stated aim is "to manage information efficiently so that [they] can provide [their] users the information that matters most to them" (Knowledge@Wharton, 2006). Determining what "matters most" to college and university students is a matter of determining the "niche demographics" of the college campus community (boyd & Ellison, 2007).

College Student Identity: Issues and Research on Online Social Networking Sites

> The Internet is not something that exists in isolation. It is a venue where interaction occurs, yet that interaction is grounded in real people...their creations...and the people who interact with that software and with other people. (Katz & Rice, 2002, p. 13)

Students on our college and university campuses today comprise a unique generation. Born after 1977, our students are typically defined by a generational culture of interaction mediated by technology. Referred to as the Net Generation, our students mediate self-expression through technology and claim creative autonomy in the communication and representation of their identities and cultures online. Eager for digital innovation that will expand the limits of expression through language and text, the Net Generation on campus has changed the narrative of identity as a consequence of their socialization through technology. They not only consume information through digital inquiry but *produce* it as well. The Net Generation college student consumes, produces, and makes meaning of social bonds and relational connections in the new real time of online communication. As a generation raised on technology, college students today have produced cultures of interactive communication and self-expression never before experienced on college campuses.

How did the college and university campus become a culture of digital communication? How did computer-mediated communication come to define campus culture in the early 21st century?

In *The Postmodern Condition: A Report on Knowledge* (1984) Jean-François Lyotard projected that the future metanarrative of self and identity would be situated in the technological. With the enhancements of technology, Lyotard anticipated that language would become ever more central in the development of social bonds or relationships, that the social bond—itself a "language game" and a "game of inquiry" (p. 15)—would rely even more on expression to be the means for information sharing, knowledge exchange, and learning. In the technological age language will *create* meaning, a challenge to modernist assumptions about the role of language in human relationships.

To say that language will create meaning is to say that language—and in the case of Facebook—computer-mediated self-expression and representation through text—is not limited by reality. In other words, language structured and positioned in and through technological spaces on social networking sites like Facebook is not bound by the regulations of explanatory theories of truth. What is scripted on Facebook may not necessarily conform to the rules of the real world, or, who I "am" on Facebook or any other social networking site is not necessarily proscribed by preexisting real-world terms. College campus culture, then, is a cultivation of those real and online individual and group identities that gain significance through recurring activities and behaviors or actions that carry symbolic weight. The sharing of information becomes ritualized, and thus norms of behavior and their significance become shared (Baym, 1998). Expression and discourse displayed in and through social networking technology, then, is a view of student identity and campus culture that may reject traditional assumptions about truth and reality, about the variability of language and reality, and the consequent unpredictability of personal and group identity. As an "engine of social relations," computer-mediated communication on social networking sites like

Facebook can disregard customary meanings of self and community (Jones, 1998).

From this perspective, technology in the 21st century is a site of "hyper-reality" (Baudrillard, 2001) in which constructed and conditional personal identity extends simultaneously beyond the real and the online space. Personal identity online plays with new forms of expression, explores possible other identities, and interacts and bonds in ways previously unanticipated. Technologically situated, online personal and group or community identity is unpredictable, changeable, imitative, often incongruous, or not. On social networking sites like Facebook, we witness the fluid alterations, adjustments, and adaptations of college students' identities—the Facebook "profile" is and *isn't* the student user. Facebook profiles can be misrepresentative though not inauthentic; students can create profiles that are mischievous, ironic, or decidedly earnest. On Facebook, identity can be simultaneously stable and alterable. Yet, the "common ground" of campus and generational culture enables the sharing of predictable signals that together with the connection to offline interactions results in the transmission of identity that is deemed authentic and trustworthy (Lampe et al., 2007).

For the current generation of college students, then, computer-mediated communication that is effortless, fast, and that supports many different types of media is commonplace. Coming of age in a technological era in which computing has always been user-friendly, personal, and used for multiple purposes, college and university students on campus today have experienced the Internet and all of its functions beginning in their early teenage years and have come to campus technologically practiced and proficient. As young adolescents, the generation of American college students born between 1984 and 1989, was likely to have used the Internet before entering college, to have owned their own computers, communicated via e-mail or Instant Messenger (IM), and experienced computer-mediated communication on the Internet as a part of their daily campus routine. Now characterized as comprising the Net Generation, college students in the 21st century benefit from the advancements in information technology during their elementary through high school years and now view such technologies as customary and conventional. As highlighted in

Educating the Net Generation (Oblinger & Oblinger, 2005), college and university students today don't necessarily learn technology; they understand it as very nearly an innate or natural condition of life. As Tapscott (1998) astutely observed of the Net Generation, "Technology is completely transparent to them" (p. 33). Net Generation graduate and undergraduate students born after 1977 have grown up in a digital world. Constituting 30% of the population in the United States, this generation is no longer tied solely to the consumption of "one-way, centralized media" (Tapscott, 1998). Rather, they produce communication that is mediated through computers and that connects them to each other. Unlike one-way media like TV, computer-mediated communication does not "atomize" this generation (Jones, 1998, p. 3).

As early adopters and heavy users, college students have positively integrated the Internet and information technology and their myriad of uses into their lives on campus. These are college and university students who use information technology intuitively, use images as a means for self-expression, and who move between real and online worlds instantly and straightforwardly (Oblinger & Oblinger, 2005). Considered visually skilled, college students also certainly use the Internet for academic tasks, such as contacting faculty, communicating with study groups, or doing library research, but they use the Internet largely as a medium for social communication (Jones, 2002). In the *ECAR Study of Undergraduates Students and Information Technology 2006* (Salaway, Katz, Caruso, Kvavik, & Nelson, 2006), for example, socializing and communicating through information technology was noted as playing a central role in the lives of undergraduates. In particular, the study's authors noted that Facebook plays "an important role in many undergraduate students' world" and that their "enthusiasm for [Facebook's] features and ability to connect with other like-minded students was very evident" (pp. 24–25). As a vehicle for college students' social communication and networking, the Internet has proven an ideal and practical utility, and like the other uses of the Internet (blogging, music downloading, etc.), social networking sites on the Internet have affected the nature and culture of campus life. Able to customize their social connections through the Internet's capabilities, students plan and organize their social relations on and off campus. As consumers, the Net Generation wants abundant options, highly customized environments, and because they are neither fearful nor timid about technology, they demand functionality (Tapscott, 1998).

Social networking sites like Facebook are a relatively recent Internet phenomenon, and they have their origins in the launching of the first major social networking sites, Classmates (1995) and SixDegrees (1997–2001). Predicated on social network theory and analysis (Freeman, 2004), these two sites were created on the supposition that a grid of an individual's social contacts and relationships could be socially and culturally relevant and thus valuable. The earlier site, Classmates, was constructed based on the idea that direct or known ties between individuals could be identified through the Internet's search technology. On Classmates, basic membership is free but a subscription price can be paid to gain access to more of the site's features. The central feature, finding former classmates from primary school through college, requires that an individual user permit an on-site Classmates search of her name so that classmates can be "found" (Classmates. com, 2008). The central principle that motivates and grounds this social networking site is that a direct, person-to-person connection or relationship exists or has existed previously in real life. As a bounded system, Classmates networks direct, real-life social ties.

With the launching of SixDegrees in 1997, social networking on the Internet added a new dimension, the social graphing of indirect social ties, connections that though not directly individual-to-individual were still relevant. SixDegrees could map all relevant connections or ties between individuals off-site as well as on-site. Based on a social circles network model, SixDegrees users ("nodes") could send text messages and post on bulletin boards to connections ("ties") at different levels. Named after John Guare's play, *Six Degrees of Separation* and the pop cultural phenomenon, the "Six Degrees of Kevin Bacon" game, and premised on the "small world problem" (Milgram, 1967), the site was the first to allow users to create profiles, construct a list of friends, browse that list, and create a complex, multinode network of ties. Sites like SixDegrees soon increased, offering various iterations of user profiles and bounded inventories of friends. Launched in 1999, LiveJournal offered users the opportunity to create journals or diaries, as well as to make commentary on events or issues. What made Live-Journal unique and a forerunner of sites like Facebook was the user's ability to follow the journal entries of friends and set her own privacy settings (boyd & Ellison, 2007). Tracking friends' communications and controlling what personal information is viewed by friends and nonfriends are features that social network sites like Facebook refined and improved consequently making these sites preferred over the earlier sites.

As a niche community or walled garden, college or university students reside in a unique relational space in which they are interdependent with both people and sociocultural institutions. Facebook appears to function as a cultural ecology not bound by rigid, traditional principles of identity and communication. On Facebook, college student identities are performed in this niche and have shared significance. How college students position or function in this online community cannot be explained by static relational positions characteristic of earlier generations. A student's "agency" on Facebook, for example, cannot be fully explained through a view of associations between objective, empirically verifiable identities. On Facebook, students need not provide verifiable evidence of whatever self or selves are posted through text or visual images, and there is no limit on how often profile information or images can be switched or altered. These are unreliable presentations of students' identities in that they demand no corroboration, no confirmation of the identity presented. Identity on Facebook appears to have the qualities of impersonation that qualifies as real. Identities through the construction of profiles often appear as cultural performances and narratives of identity that is part fiction, part real-life. Much like gender is in the postmodern sense an imitation of what is assumed as the real (Butler, 1990, p. viii), a student's identity on Facebook is a cultural performance not necessarily regulated by traditional forms. Facebook profiles are often constructed to exercise nonrational forces and present or perform a "repertoire of potentials" (Gergen, 1991). Taking place on Facebook is a self-determination that is interdependent and relational and that appears to reconfigure and reconstitute the composition of community culture on campus. Facebook's asynchronous and virtual communication constructs not the conventional face-to-face community, but a world of social transactions that defy the conventional conception of individuals looking inward for self-definition. On Facebook, self appears to look outward just as much or more than it looks inward. Self moves across varied and multiple group memberships with the aim of creating a set of connections, a network of relationships that help define the individual. The traditional separation of Self and Other is tested on Facebook, as each is simultaneously the other many times over with no end in sight. Facebook "friends" is constitutive of whatever self (or aspect of self) is performed and the interpretation of the viewer—whether a consensual viewer or browsing voyeur.

On Facebook, students function in what Gergen (1991) has called the "floating worlds" of 21st century technologies that have no specific geographic location, varying criteria for membership, and little (if any) control by external authorities. The students in our study do and don't acknowledge external authority—those actors peripheral to this cultural niche. They change and don't change their relationships and presentations of self as a response to the intrusion of authority, and construct highly complex and not categorically rational rules to subvert the disturbance of and interference by authority.

Since its development in 2004, Facebook use by young adults has been a frequent topic of reporting by the popular media. Described as a "giant word of mouth engine" by Wired.com, the popular online periodical that covers technology's impact (Vogelstein, 2007), Facebook has received the attention of journalists worldwide, with most of the focus on user identity and authenticity. The popular press has documented the impact that Facebook has had on user privacy and the determination of attributable behavior, as well as broader sociocultural concerns about its use by young adults. The Associated Press has reported on "threat assessment groups" developed on college and university campuses in which student affairs and counseling administrators, law enforcement and faculty monitor Facebook profiles for signs of troubled students (McMurray, 2008). A response to recent shootings on American campuses, these groups aim to discern signals of emotional and mental distress on students' Facebook profiles or entries that they post on other students' walls. National Public Radio has reported on the Cedar Fest student "riot" at Michigan State University (Millich, 2008), noting that the party had been promoted on

Facebook. Subsequent news stories in national dailies, campus week-lies, and other professional periodicals like the *Chronicle of Higher Education* have reported on Facebook's liability for the damages that resulted from the Cedar Fest-MSU student unrest (Rampell, 2008). College and university administrator monitoring of student behavior and the issues that it raises is a frequent topic appearing in Inside-highered.com. Reporting on the development of YouDiligence.com, a social network monitoring service aimed at policing student ath-lete behavior on Facebook (Powers, 2008), this online news source for higher education worldwide described the administrative appeal of such sites. The *New York Times* has featured articles on how cam-pus law enforcement departments keep an eye on underaged student alcohol consumption by cyber-patrolling party planning on Facebook (Hass, 2006); articles on college students using Facebook for political action and campaigning (Stelter, 2008); reporting on parental screen-ing of their children's college roommate selections by viewing Face-book profiles (Lewin, 2006); and has covered concerns over speech codes and hate speech issues on Facebook (Cohen, 2007a). In Decem-ber of 2007, CNN media outlets aired a story, "Girls Gone Facebook" investigating the Facebook group, "Thirty Reasons Girls Should Call It a Night." As reported on CNN, a group with over 172,000 mem-bers, "Thirty Reasons Girls Should Call It a Night" posts photographs of college women consuming alcohol, getting drunk, and engaging in problematic behavior (Cohen, 2007a). Stories about potential employ-ers vetting job applicants through Facebook are now ubiquitous in college and university student newspapers. The *Stanford Daily* (Fuller, 2006) and the *Minnesota Daily* (Rozwadowski, 2007), for example, warned their university students to use caution when posting pho-tos of themselves on Facebook because of potential discrimination by future employers. Early in Facebook's history, nationally and inter-nationally circulating newspapers like the *Christian Science Monitor* warned its readers about employer screening and the public nature of profiles (Lupsa, 2006). A study conducted by University of Dayton researchers in 2007 suggested that the majority of employers surveyed (83%) believe it ethical to check the Facebook profiles of job appli-cants before making candidates offers of employment (Read, 2007). And with Facebook's fastest growing demographic consisting of users

35 years or older (Grossman, 2007, p. 54), parents can also enter the network despite their children's consternation over their breech of generational territory limits (Slatalla, 2007).

Much as the popular press has focused its attention on the relationship between student behavior and authenticity, academic scholarship and research has attempted to gain a richer and deeper understanding of the online social network phenomenon and its consequences. As catalogued by boyd and Ellison (2007), much of the academic research on social networking sites like Facebook has focused on the anthropology and sociology of social networks and their construction, arrangement, and organization; the psychology of self-representation and authenticity; the interaction effects between online and offline relationships; and the potential danger to users and their privacy concerns.

In the late 1990s much of the research and scholarly work on computer-mediated communication examined the nature of social relations online. Newly understood as a space in which individual identities could be embedded and in which social connections could be made, accounts of the conception of "cyberspace" attempted to identify and examine the consequences for the creation and recreation of communities in virtual space. Communications, media studies, and other interdisciplinary faculty along with researchers from the social and behavioral sciences, began to explore the assumptions, meanings, and effects of presenting and constructing self-identity online. In 1995, the edited volume, *CyberSociety 2.0: Computer-Mediated Communication and Community* presented scholarly assessments of "cybersociety," which included the pioneering work of Nancy Baym (1998), "The Emergence of Community in Computer-Mediated Communication." Attending to the nature of online communities that were topic specific and not the niche communities of social networking sites that would develop years later, Baym and other contributors critically examined the meanings and implications of social arrangements that emerge from new technologies, especially those online groups that were subject-specific or topic-specific online communities. Contributors to the volume concerned themselves with sociopsychology of computer-mediated communication, the cultures that were developing among Internet users, and the nature of online relationships and their effects on real life social bonds. Predating the niche specific, bounded network sites that like Facebook rely on preexisting social relationships and connections in the real world, these early scholarly assessments of online sociality did not anticipate the fluid nature of online social networking sites. Baym's updating in 1998 of her initial consideration three years earlier, still characterized "online communities" as achieving community status solely online. As Baym observed, online communities become "communities" as a consequence of their computer-mediated communications. The Internet is the space in which the community comes into being. Baym astutely observed, however, that these online communities were shaped by real world factors.

In noting the appropriation of "external contexts, temporal structure, system infrastructure, group purposes, and participant characteristics," Baym (1998, p. 51) anticipated the research shift that was necessary with the rise of social networking sites predicated on preexisting, real world communities. SixDegrees, Friendster, MySpace, and Facebook presented researchers and scholars with a new form of computer-mediated communication—virtual interactions among individuals in preexisting communities, among users who already knew each other or had some form of preexisting, real-world social connection. The real-world communities of schools, colleges, and generational membership were now online and their communication was context-driven, bounded by shared events and knowledge, and ordered by the sites' infrastructure itself predicated on the assumed needs, behaviors, and proclivities of individual members and existing community standards.

Early scholarship on the production of self and identity through computer-mediated communication largely focused on the metaphysics of individuation online or how individual real-world identity would transfer to virtual spaces. Informed by Kenneth Gergen's (1991) conceptualization of the postmodern identity as "saturated self" and Charles Taylor's (1992) critique of modernity's construction of an abstract, decontextualized self, much of the scholarly treatment of online identity involved philosophical questions or psychological deliberations. Emirbayer and Goodwin's (1994) sociological critique of early network analysis suggested that research about these nascent sites took culture and "human agency" for granted and in doing so, could not adequately postulate the effects of "subjective meaning and motivation" (p. 1413). Did real-world self-recognition transfer to online subjectivities? How? Taylor's (1992) "horizons of meaning" suggested that the significant conditions of social relations and communication with others were an essential characteristic of human communities. Scholars examining the problems of personal identity online had to consider whether or how these "horizons of meaning" were transported to online sites. Thus, the question of computer-mediated online identity was one that had to reflect on the set of psychological, social, and historic properties that constituted off-line, real-world identity, and then consider whether the move online was informed by these properties. For example, in 1996 *Computer Mediated Communication Magazine* dedicated its March issue to women's participation in cyberspace, highlighting the recent publications on the same topic: *Life on the Screen: Identity in the Age of the Internet* (Turkle, 1995), *Nattering on the Net: Women, Power, and Cyberspace* (Spender, 1996), and *NetChick: A Smart-Girl Guide to the Wired World* (Sinclair, 1995). The assumption made in these texts was that gender in real-world sociocultural structures and thus identity was salient and as a result it was plausible that it would be significant online. In the early years of social networks, researchers like DeVoss and Selfe (2002) set out to examine this assumption by studying how college women shaped their online identities on home pages as a function of gender, but still had not factored the dynamic nature of identity on networked niche communities online. In the ensuing years, the innovation and improved technological capability and social networking capacity would require researchers and scholars to scrutinize the impact of the properties of identity differently.

Self-presentation, its authenticity and execution, was a key focus of early social networking research. Between the initial launching of SixDegrees in 1997 and Facebook in 2004, social networking sites like LiveJournal (1998), AsianAvenue (1999), LunarStorm (2000), MiGente (2000), Friendster (2002) and MySpace (2003) had signaled a change in online communication. Taking note of the change in the landscape of online communities, academic researchers began to focus their attention on how users negotiated self-presentation on sites premised on preexisting social relations. The "subjective meaning and motivation" that informed a user's online self-presentation argued earlier by Emirbayer and Goodwin (1994) was by the early years of online social networking a central consideration for researchers.

Prior to the explosion of social networking sites based on preexisting friendships and social connections, researchers focused their attention on Internet use in general and its consequences. Katz and Rice (2002) in their influential text, *Social Consequences of Internet Use: Access, Involvement and Interaction*, chronicled the first national random study of the social consequences of Internet use among Americans, identifying access to civic and community involvement, social interaction and expression as the central concerns of Internet research (p. 4). Their "Syntopia Project" attempted to chart Internet behavior from 1996 through 2000 through a sequence of random telephone interviews. Arguing that the existing literature on Internet use conceptualized Internet use and its consequences as "too extreme" (p. 13), Katz and Rice instead argued for a "syntopian" conceptualization, recognizing from their project's data that the Internet is also virtual space in which people "interact, express themselves, emote, and find new friends" (p. xxi).

Thus, the dystopian views of Internet use (that there is a lack of authenticity, that negative consequences define its use-value, that time spent on virtual sociality is time taken away from real-life social activities, and that attempts at communities online were depersonalizing and homogenizing) (p. 10) and the "utopian" views (that the Internet's use value is that it enables us to make friends and stay in touch with friends and family more regularly and that identity is archived) (p. 11) failed to capture the interactive nature of the experience. Further, such dichotomization of its use-value ignored the fact that the virtual spaces do not exist in isolation from the real-life experiences of its designers and users, and perhaps more importantly, that such a view overlooked the fact that the Internet "facilitates social capital through collective interaction more than it fosters introversion through individual information seeking" (p. 203). Katz and Rice observed that participants in the Syntopia Project perceived their personal home pages not as disjointed self-representation but as integrated, albeit "one-sided personal introductions" (p. 277). Self or identity presented online by contributors to the Syntopia surveys was not assumed to be disembodied, nor were cyber interactions. Rather, the nature of identity online, its structure and construction, was secured to real-world social relations and in a challenge to postmodern concerns over the fragmentation of identity online, the researchers discovered that in actuality, the Internet "has a tendency" to unify aspects of self more so than not (p. 283).

By the early years of the 21st century, then, Internet use was being investigated in more complex ways, though the governing agenda continued to be identifying the demography of user identity and their use. In particular, research focused on the patterns and effects of Internet use. In 2000 the Pew Internet and American Life Project began its long-term research endeavor to inventory and record the impact of the Internet on American life when they gathered data on health care online, new users since 1998, women's particular uses of the Internet, the growing "digital divide," and emerging trust and privacy issues. In 2002, Pew reported data on parents' Internet use and the rise of search engines, and specifically targeted the college-aged population in its reports, "The Internet Goes to College" and "College Students on the Web" (Jones, 2002; Rainie, Kalehoff, & Hess, 2002). In 2004, Instant Messenger (IM) use was examined, as was the emergent phenomenon of wireless computer readiness. Two years later, Pew researchers chronicled podcast downloading, blogging, cell phones, online dating, and "surfing for fun." Pew's "The Future of the Internet II" (Anderson & Rainie, 2006), gathered the speculations on the scope and impact of the Internet by 2020 from influential Internet leaders, advocates, and analysts. In the same year, Pew researchers studied the strength of Internet ties and concluded that the Internet and e-mail positively affected real-life social bonds. Generational use indices were also catalogued that same year.

But by 2007 and 2008, The Pew Internet and American Life Project began to note the trends in teenage/adolescent and late-adolescent use of social networking media and like other researchers, embarked on a series of projects to ascertain the frequency and value of use among this age cohort (Lenhart, Madden, Rankin Macgill, & Smith, 2007). Concerns about "cyberbullying" and contacts with strangers online were the centerpieces in this effort, though Pew also turned its view to new developments like online video, and identity-specific community use in "Latinos Online" (Fox & Livingston, 2007). By 2008, Pew's publications focused on video sharing and mobile access (Horrigan, 2008).

In concert with the Pew Internet studies, research conducted by EDUCAUSE Center for Applied Research (ECAR) beginning in 2004 presented a focused, composite picture of undergraduate students' use of technology (Kvavik & Caruso, 2004). Grounded in the data that identified the college-going population as "digital cognoscenti" and "digital connoisseurs" (Salaway et al., 2006, p. 5), the ECAR study began as an inventory of students' technology use and evolved into a continuing survey of student technological preferences and behaviors. Reinforcing existing data on the rate and type of Internet use among college and university students throughout the first two years of the study (e.g., Cooperative Institutional Research Program) by 2007 ECAR had constructed a portrait of campus life that included an overwhelmingly daily, mobile, wireless college student user who primarily uses technology for communication (Salaway et al., 2007). New to the findings was the significant emergence of social networking use among undergraduates, especially among younger students since 2004 (p. 14). ECAR's data (Kvavik & Caruso, 2005) had reported that 69.7% of undergraduates used social networking sites but by 2007, use had increased almost 20%. According to ECAR 2007 data, 81.6% of college and university undergraduates use social networking sites and "younger students report more frequent engagement in these activities" (Salaway et al., 2007, p. 12). Students participating in ECAR 2007 focus made it clear, however, that their use of computer-mediated communication technologies like Instant Messenger and Facebook, were not a part of their academic culture on campus and in fact, they preferred that these social communication technologies "remain in the scope of their private lives" (p. 14). Students especially do not want faculty on social networking sites, the inference being that sites like Facebook are the province of students and their social relationships. The salience of both the centrality of social networking sites and their use by undergraduates has prompted ECAR researchers to next study social networking among college students, with a special focus on Facebook, and other social, interactive technology like multiuser virtual environments (MUVEs) and massively multiplayer online games (MMOGs) (p. 17).

Within the expanding, multidisciplinary literature on computer mediated communication and social networking in the last few years, and of particular relevance to Facebook and the college-going student, is the research and scholarship specifically focused on adolescent and late-adolescent Internet use, and studies that shed light on self-representation and identity construction, and the culture of campus relations. Flowers, Pascarella, and Pierson (2000) attempted to examine the connection between first year college students' Internet use and their cognitive outcomes. Though Flowers et al. did find differences between two-year and four-year college users, overall no significant effect on cognition was determined. Anderson's (2001) exploratory study of 1,300 college students and their Internet use suggested an "overuse" phenomenon among this age group, and that approximately 10% of Internet-using students sampled have used the Internet to the degree that their use meets criteria of other forms of addiction. Malaney (2004–2005) studied undergraduate Internet use at a large public university and like Anderson (2001) concluded that about 10% of users exhibit problematic behaviors related to overuse, and that men spent more time than women on the Internet. However, Malaney's (2004–2005) data also suggested that the development of identity and meaningful relationships was cited as a reason for Internet use. Laird and Kuh (2005) identified the relationship between productive Internet use and an undergraduate's engagement with learning and the larger campus milieu. Suggesting a strong positive relationship between academic Internet use and collaborative learning, Laird and Kuh also speculated that student Internet use could also increase the likelihood for other forms of engagement.

Research interest in college student Internet use and their computer mediated communication was largely due to their generational particularity and higher rates of use relative to the general population. In the Pew Internet and American Life Project reports, *College Students and the Web* (Rainie et al., 2002) and *The Internet Goes to College: How Students are Living in the Future with Today's Technology* (Jones, 2002) researchers identified the particular Internet interests of college students and the characteristics of their computer-mediated communication. In the latter report, findings suggested that under-graduates use the Internet primarily for convenient social communi-cation, and that they expect ubiquitous access to online environments. Predating the mainstreaming of social network sites on college and university campuses, this particular study highlighted students' use of e-mail to communicate with other students (on-campus or at other campuses) and with faculty, the use of Instant Messenger (IM) as a means to communicate with friends, and students' generally positive experiences with Internet use. Though implied by these Pew stud-ies, college student Internet use also carried with it the social con-text and "horizons of meaning" (Taylor, 1992) that intrigued scholars interested in understanding the sociopsychology of student life. For example, Lanthier and Windham (2004) wondered whether gender moderated the correlations between Internet use and college adjust-ment, a study that combined the demographic characteristics of use with the psychology of use in late-adolescence. Grounding their work on constructs of emerging adulthood (Arnett, 2000), Lanthier and Windham (2004) identified gender as a moderating variable but only so among male students, and noted that overall, what is important for adjustment to college relative to Internet use is not the time spent online but rather "the manner in which the time is spent and the feel-ings and experiences associated with that time" (p. 602). The fact that college men's adjustment was positively associated with Internet use led the researchers to speculate that in the cyber world men can "step outside gender stereotypes that can restrict emotional openness and expressiveness" (p. 602).

Thus, by the ushering in of the era of MySpace and Facebook, aca-demic and scholarly research has focused principally on the rate and demography of Internet use with some forays into the psychology of identity and use, especially among college-aged students.

Early in the life of the Internet, Jordan (1999) observed that at the individual level the Internet's "power" had to do with the fact that our identities are reinforced every time we communicate online. Identities online seem to reflect some measure of the user's agency and author-ity over self-expression and self-promotion. Online, our identities can and cannot be distinguished from what they are in reality; we can be as authentic or as counterfeit as we wish online. In the case of social networking sites, these virtual spaces don't appear to be understood as "hyper-reality" in the sense that what is real is indistinguishable from what is fake (Baudrillard, 1983). Rather, identity on sites like Facebook seems predicated on the assumption of authenticity and the authority of the individual user to control its production and consumption scaffolded by cultural customs and conventions. Identity as produced and consumed on social networks is tempered and bounded by cultural norms but can also transgress real life restrictions. Not only unrestricted by the limits of physical space and geography, online identity can be exaggerated or understated, and can break and comply with sociocultural rules. Identity online is also temporal in that its consumption and production is both synchronic (at one moment) and diachronic (over a period of time).

What about relationships online? Historically, we have understood the nature of human relations as being secured by the ethics, psychology, and anthropology of real life associations between and among discrete individuals, between and among individuals in specifically defined or loosely defined groups, and to some extent, as affinity among individuals in "imagined communities" in which face-to-face, direct interaction between members is not assured (Anderson, 1998). Online relationships seem to present each of these conditions, perhaps reconstituted by the capabilities of technology. But early research on Internet relationality focused less on the prospect of new forms of relationships and identities occurring online and more on their precise distinctions in real-life versus "virtual" life. Perhaps, as Slater (2002) argues, we may find that online relationality is a "co-presence" analogous to face-to-face exchanges (p. 536). Real-world interactions occur in an actual, physical space but online, the absence of spatial certainty may alter how identities are consumed and produced. How individuals relate to each other online, then, must capture identity in real space and virtual space, as well as preexisting relationality and its new constitution online. Social and behavioral science research on social networking sites has been dedicated primarily to examining and understanding the nature of relationships and on the production and consumption of identity in the networks.

Characterized by boyd and Ellison (2007) as "impression management" the idea that certain information is a signal or indicator of something that identifies the online user characterizes the research on social networking sites relative to identity creation and interpretation. Early work by Donath (1999) explored the nature of identity authenticity and profile signals online in Usenet, a public, threaded discussion system. Donath concluded that though users signal particular identity characteristics, they need not necessarily possess these personality or physical traits in the real world. Enhancing or concealing aspects of identity were not very costly to users and in fact, users accepted a certain level of identity counterfeiting as a function of online communication. However, in early social networking sites where profiles were static, a balance between truth and fiction was likely in user profiles. As boyd (2004) noted about Friendster users, self-presentations are often a "balance" between privacy and self-disclosure. On Friendster specifically, user authenticity and identity trustworthiness was challenged by the construction of fake profiles known as "Fakesters." These bogus personalities confused many users and undermined the trust in the network. Unable at times to figure out what or who was "real," Friendster user confidence in Friendster network connections was challenged (boyd, 2004). In contrast, Facebook's correspondence to real, preexisting connections within a particular community (college or university affiliation) assures some measure of authenticity, or at least some measure of validity. On Facebook, profile information can be more readily confirmed than in other online networks precisely because identity can be verified by previous association or future offline encounters. Because Facebook users have a shared set of social connections, the accuracy and legitimacy of identity claims can be easier to ascertain than on relatively unbounded communities, like MySpace. Identity on Facebook need not only be serious or "true to life"; irony and playfulness are acceptable misrepresentations of self (Lampe et al., 2007).

Identity and its authenticity is also shaped by user agency or the degree to which users feel that they can control their profile information, and as a result have authority over what information about themselves is made public and what information remains private. Static or fixed profiles like those on Friendster did not unfetter user agency so that self-presentation was largely unchanging. But in social network sites like Facebook in which users actively create and recreate profiles, user agency is restricted only by the confines of site developers and technology (Marwick, 2005). That said it is also true that social networking sites are archival and permit surveillance so that a user's ability to control privacy—or to be an agent in the consumption of their online identity—is ambiguous (Barnes, 2006). By definition, social networking sites are also spaces in which self-presentation can be revealed by other users in the network; that is, "friends" can make public comments about the user that can be seen by other users in the network. Despite the fact that Facebook users can control who is allowed to see profile information, it is none the less true that once permission is granted, information previously held private by the profile user can be made public. The assumption of privacy by online social network users is predicated on the trust ascribed to the other network users. In the case of Facebook, because network users are "friends" or at least "friends" of "friends," some measure of trust is assumed and consequently, user self-presentation is believed to be governed by the user. User agency—defined by the degree to which their authenticity and privacy is maintained—is assumed on Facebook.

Online social networking sites are by design "egocentric" in that the individual user is at the center of her social network or social graph (boyd & Ellison, 2007, p. 9). Self-representation is a central emphasis on these sites, and as in the case of Facebook, that self-representation can feature photographs, lists of music and movie preferences, political affiliations, videos of users themselves, or by proxies who illustrate something that the user deems relevant to her identity. Profiles are user portrayals of how users understand self and how it is that they may want to be seen by other users. But as Rosen (2007) points out in her critique of the "new narcissism" that has arisen in social network sites, sites like Facebook may not enable users to "attain what [the site] promises—a surer sense of who we are and where we belong" (¶ 4). Rosen argues that the demands to expand friendship connections and to self-represent on social networking sites motivate users to set themselves apart from other users, or even to compete with "friends" by engaging in "coarseness and vulgarity" or "exhibitionism." This principle persisted in Donath and boyd's (2004) examination of the public display of connections on online social networks sites. Donath and boyd concluded that as the "most salient feature" of online social networking sites, making public user relationships and associations, is an "implicit verification of identity" (pp. 72–73). Though unnoted in Donath and boyd's (2004) examination, Rosen's (2007) concern that social networking sites may have negative effects on self-worth because users essentially "market" themselves online, is articulated in Valkenburg and Schouten (2006). They investigated the consequences of online social networking sites like MySpace on self-worth and happiness among 10- to 19-year-olds and concluded that positive responses to user profiles improved social self-esteem and well-being, whereas negative feedback decreased both measures. Ellison, Steinfield, and Lampe's (2007) examination of the benefits of Facebook use did find that users with low self-esteem and low life satisfaction experienced positive outcomes from use. Walther, Van der Heide, Kim, Westerman, and Tom Tong (2008) explored how messages placed on Facebook profiles (on the "Wall" feature) affected other viewers' perceptions of the profile owner, and how the physical attractiveness of "friends" signaled the profile owner's attractiveness and authenticity. Finding that profile owners' friends' attractiveness affected their own in an "assimilative pattern," the researchers implicitly endorsed Rosen's (2007) concern that social networking sites encourage a new brand of self-promotion and egotism historically not assumed central to friendship or social connection. Additionally, Marwick's (2005) examination of self-presentation, authenticity, and power in social networking sites suggests that the social networking sites like Facebook encourage accrual of superficial or one-dimensional connections effectively commodifying the relationships. Once commodified, argues Marwick (2005), these online relationships become social capital. On MySpace, for example, boyd (2007) noted that because friends are displayed on an individual's profile page, these connections serve to signal significant information about the profile owner. As boyd astutely suggests, other users will then make judgments about the profile owner based on who these friends are, and that "group identities form around and are reinforced by the collective tastes and attitudes of those who identify with the group. Online, this cue is quite helpful in enabling people to find their bearings" (2007, p. 13). Identity on social networking sites, then, is also a function of the audience or at least, the "imagined audience" that like "imagined communities" have shared ideals, values, and expectations, and in which individual users can be validated by their peers (boyd, 2007).

A benefit, then, of social networking "friends" is the formation and maintenance of some forms of social capital. As findings from research conducted by Ellison et al. (2007) suggest, Facebook use can help undergraduate students both amass and bridge social capital. Undergraduate participants in this study reported that their primary use of Facebook was to communicate with high school friends and college friends on their campus. The extension of the social graph on Facebook effectively increases the social capital of users because the more ties that are made, the greater the likelihood that users will trade on their associations in the real world, either on campus or as alumni. But social capital garnered through Facebook use according to these researchers does not improve "bonding social capital." In other words, though social capital increases with increased connections, these are not deep, emotionally rich relationships.

Given that preexisting relationships are the underpinning of social networking sites like Facebook, and that the site is organized around a particular community, it would stand to reason that gender, racial, ethnic, and social class identity would be factors and have some effect on self-representation. Little research has been done to ascertain the effects of racial, ethnic, or class identity on online social networking. Though some gender effects have been noted in disparate research (e. g., boyd, 2004, 2007; EDUCAUSE, 2007; Ellison et al., 2007; Valkenburg & Schouten, 2006), as of this writing a thorough examination of the effects of gender on self-presentation, "impression management" (boyd & Ellison, 2007), and the cultivation of social capital on online social networking sites has not been conducted. The same can be said of the effects of racial and ethnic identity, as well as social or economic class identification. Though boyd (2007) found that race and social class played little role in terms of access to social networking sites by 14- to 18-year-olds, Hargittai (2007) has asserted that among college students, race and ethnicity are associated with social networking site use. For example, Hargittai contends that Latino students are more likely to use MySpace and that Asian and Asian-American students are less likely to do so. The contention in Hargittai's findings is that ethnic, racial, and class backgrounds correlate with the selection of particular sites, or that particular sites resonate with distinct populations of users. In our study, as in Hargittai's work, race and ethnicity did predict social networking site choice, and as was also true in the Hargittai study, parents' educational level (a proxy for social class) also was predictive of site choice. Associated with these findings is the participation of Asian, Black, and Latino youth ages 16 to 24 on sites dedicated specifically to ethnic and racial groups. AsianAvenue, BlackPlanet, and MiGente are each sites devoted to users who identify racially and ethnically with the sites' community. These sites, according to Byrne (2008), are racialized public spaces in which and through which adolescents and young adults can make connections, strengthen their cultural identities, navigate the public and private dimensions of race and ethnicity, and to some extent, advance intragroup communication.

We can confidently say, then, that the Net Generation, which Tapscott (1998) identified in the late 1990s, has developed technologically and now claims online social networking as the space in which and through which they "see people, information, games, applications, services, friends and protagonists" (p. 39). The synchronic and diachronic nature of their identities and interactions on these sites make them central characters in their virtual self-production as well as supporting characters in the virtual networked community. On online social network sites like Facebook, this generation of college students draws from the existing sociology of campus life *and* modifies, extends, and archives the patterns of interactions and relationships and constitution of campus cultures. Social networking sites like Facebook are for this generation of college and university students a fundamental component of their lived experiences, and an important element of the phenomenology of campus culture.

3

STUDENTS SPEAK

Campus Culture, Identity, and Facebook

In our view, the authenticity of the "hybrid environments" of social networking sites (Ruhleder, 2000) on campus can best be presented by listening to the voices of students. The nature of online campus culture is such that any investigation of these spaces really demands an ethnographic presentation of their meaning to students as interpreted by the students themselves. Students' explanations of text and images, and their understanding of the purposes and functions of social networking provide us with a more extensive view of student online behavior, and more importantly, the significance that online social networking has for students' college experience. In many ways, the following ethnographic portraits of four residential college students—Kris, Matthew, Teresa, and Jordan[1]—are representative of the sociology of social networking among young, collegiate adults. Their accounts of online campus culture are vetted through epistemological positions informed by their race and ethnicity, gender identification, sexuality, class year, and other individual and group characteristics. Illustrative of the ways in which online campus culture is developed, enacted, and resisted, these young women and men talk about the differences between men's and women's uses of Facebook; how they understand racial consciousness enacted online; how they engage in online impression management; and what meaning they make of their online voyeurism.

We highlight these particular students for many reasons. Three of these four undergraduates attend colleges originally networked in Facebook, thereby constituting online social networking as a factor in campus culture as early as 2004. Kris, Matthew, Teresa, and Jordan represent aspects of the diversity of students on these residential

43

campuses, each bringing to the conversation a distinctively individual and group-identified perspective on online campus culture. In many ways, each of these students is a witness who can explain and interpret online campus culture. Their testimonies about impression management, the production and consumption of race, ethnicity, and sexuality online, and their individual accounts of online social networking signals and symbols, provide us with an insider's view of online campus culture. Students' individual testimonies are informed by the multidimensional character of their experiences in their social locations, and as such give us a point of departure from which to understand online campus culture much more deeply. Their ethnographic portraits are representative of the complexity of each individual's life experiences and are not meant as universal decrees. That said we chose these particular students' testimonies because they are especially representative of the views of students surveyed and interviewed for this book. Kris, Matthew, Teresa, and Jordan, though they are not composites of all of the students who participated in the research, their accounts certainly exemplify the central and overriding themes found across the students in our study. In some cases, we include the testimonies of other students to widen and deepen the view of online campus culture. Hence, through the observations and testimonies of a Latina student, or a gay African-American student, or a White female student we are able to mine the reality of online campus culture and in doing so come to a better and more constructive understanding of the phenomenon.

Before presenting the portraits of Teresa, Matthew, Jordan, and Kris, we first present an overview of Facebook use—the nuts and bolts—and then briefly discuss some of the findings from our study's survey and interview data.

Facebook Primer

In order to more fully appreciate students' understanding of the role that Facebook plays in campus culture, it's first important to be aware of the central features and operations of this online social networking site. Here we present an overview of the key elements and features of the site but suggest readers deepen their knowledge of the site's capabilities by consulting the myriad of online Facebook tutorials or such texts as *Facebook: The Missing Manual* (Vander Veer, 2008). At the conclusion of this book, we also provide a glossary of terms to help newcomers to Facebook. We have chosen to highlight what seem to be the main features of this social networking site, but developers regularly change the features on Facebook, usually launching a significant development once every quarter or so.

A social networking site with user privacy as a central concern, Facebook enables users to construct a user-controlled "profile" page. The Facebook profile is the user's webpage and contains as much information as the user is willing to input. Though some skeletal information is necessary to start a profile, the user produces her profile page deciding which information will be viewed by which other Facebook users, as well as what applications will become part of her Facebook profile. Users will utilize Facebook accounts to look up and search for current friends, contact and search for old friends, and be contacted or searched for by other Facebook users. To construct a Facebook profile, users log onto the Facebook site and begin a very easy sign-up process. A new user will be asked to submit her full name, e-mail address, a new Facebook password, and month, day, and year of birth.

When users register on Facebook, they have an option to join a network. Networks can be colleges, high schools, places of employment, or geographic locations such as cities or countries. Users can choose to have everyone on Facebook be able to access their profiles, members of their network, or just their friends. When one joins a particular network, her profile is open for that entire network to see; this is the default setting. To tighten security, the user must adjust privacy settings and limit who can view her profile. Users will receive friend requests—other users will solicit them to add them to their list of friends and to allow access to their profile if their profile is limited to friends only. Facebook users can control who can have access to their personal information and who cannot by deciding which friends to add and how much information in their profiles they will let the friends see. When users receive a friend request, users can confirm or ignore the requests. Users can also choose to reveal only certain aspects of their profile to different friends. This is called a limited profile. Once on Facebook, users can send and receive messages posted on the user's personal Wall, plan and organize events, update and be updated on friends' activities and changes in their profile information (through the News Feed), play games, buy and sell things, and engage in employment networking activities. Facebook users are also able to "unfriend" or remove friends from their list of friends (and thus prevent them from having access to their profile page if their profile is for friends only). Like all other Facebook features, "unfriending" another user is a rather simple process and rarely socially loaded unless someone unfriends another as a consequence of real-world actions. Users are also able to "poke" other Facebook users to solicit communication. A digital nudge, poking can be ignored by clicking the "remove poke" icon, or can be reciprocated by clicking "poke back." All Facebook members can be poked by any other Facebook user but poking enables access to the user's Profile for one week unless the user specifies otherwise. Poke messages appear when the pokee signs into Facebook, only the user can see these messages. If the user returns the poke he receives a reminder that a return poke opens the user's profile to the poker. Some students engage in "poke wars," with groups mass poking or individual-to-individual poking.

Creating a Facebook profile is an easy, user-friendly process. Users can produce a profile page that is rudimentary or that is more elaborate and rich. Profile construction begins with entry of "basic" information: sex, date of birth, hometown, political views, and religious views. All or none of these can be entered or be made visible to other users. "Contact" information—user's e-mail, phone numbers, AIM screen name, address, and webpage—is also controlled in the same way by the user. Users can then indicate their "relationship status" choosing from "single," "in a relationship," "engaged," "married," "it's complicated," and "in an open relationship." Users then choose either "men" "women" or both in the "interested in" field and indicate if they are "looking for," "friendship," "a relationship," "dating," or "networking" (other options used to be "random play" and "whatever I can get," but the developers have since removed these). A more detailed personalization of the Facebook profile can be constructed under "personal." Here, users can free-write responses to "activities," "interests," "favorite music," "favorite TV shows," "favorite movies," "favorite books," "favorite quotes," and "about me." If someone clicks on one of the items listed in this category, all other people in that network who have the same item listed will be brought up on a list. The Education drop-down menu allows users to enter colleges attended and their academic concentration, institutional e-mail address for network-ing, and high school information. In order to be in an educational or workplace network, one must have an e-mail from that organization to verify that one belongs in that network. Regional networks do not require proof of membership in that category. Employment informa-tion under "work" explains where the user is employed, the duration of their employment, and a job description. Finally, users can upload a JPG, JIF, or PNG file to the "picture" page. This is the profile picture that will appear on the user's profile page. It is also possible, though not as accepted, to do without a profile picture. In place of a picture, a question mark appears. Users can choose to have their profile pictures appear in searches for their name or choose to have their profile pic-tures visible only to their friends.

The central user-to-user communication feature of the Facebook profile page is "the Wall." Facebook's "Wall" feature is a display of communication between Facebook friends. On the Wall friends share photos, messages, videos, links, and other communication about almost anything. The Wall functions much like a multimedia mes-sage board that is continuously updated but that is public to all friends who are given access. Thus, like all public message boards, communi-cation can be read by all who can view the Wall. A user can delete a post on his own wall or a message he posted on another friend's wall. By clicking on "Wall-to-Wall," a user can view the history of com-munication with his friend, or just click on "Write on [Friend's Name] Wall" to respond without reviewing the history.

In order to have access to other Facebook user Profiles, a user must be a member of that Facebook Network and be given access by the user. A Network is determined simply by a user's location or e-mail address. The user's college, high school, employer, or other location designated by an e-mail address constitutes the network. When a user joins a network, he will get instant access to the Facebook profiles of other network users that are not friend-restricted, the network's events, and other listings. Under the drop-down "Join a Network," users can browse and click the networks that match the users' valid e-mail addresses entered. Though changing networks is certainly permitted, Facebook will limit the number of times networks are changed as a means to detect online fraud. On MySpace users find that they can customize their pages a great deal. Unlike MySpace, however, Facebook maintains a standard Profile account view but allow users to customize many aspects and elements of their Profiles. Users can modify their Profiles by hiding Applications or sections of their Profile; they can change the position of sections on their Profile pages.

Facebook Applications, now numbering over 25,000, allow users to add built-in programs or "widgets" that provide additional information about the user or that enable the user to connect to other similarly minded users. Among the possibilities are Facebook's own applications, Groups, Events, Photos, and Marketplace, and third-party developed applications that are social, political, religious and spiritual, humorous, commercial, or philanthropic in nature. Many are simply for fun and frivolity, while others are more serious and aim to connect employers to job-seekers or vice versa, develop and generate activity for grass-roots or other political movements, and others are utility applications, such as apartment seekers. Facebook's Application directory lists its ever-growing Applications by category headings and allows users to add, edit, and delete applications easily. Facebook users are made aware that installing third-party Applications gives designers and corporate owners permission to use the personal information included in their Profiles.

One of the more popular Facebook-developed Applications is Photos. A user can create a photo "Album" very simply by clicking the Photos icon on her Profile page, and then proceed through the user-friendly fields to name, describe, and locate the photos in the Album. Most importantly, users are asked to determine to whom the Album can be visible: "Everyone," "My Networks and Friends," "People at [My Network] and Friends," "Friends of Friends," "Only Friends," and a "Customize" set of options. Users can "Customize" the viewing access to exclude users by writing in the names of users under "Except These People." A user can label her photos or "tag" them with a virtual marker by entering "Edit Album" and then using the cursor to indicate the section of the photo that will be "tagged." Clicking the cursor opens a dialog box in which the user can type the name of the person or location or item tagged and then choose to send the photo as a tagged message to other users. Users can also "untag" photos by deleting their name from the photograph, thus removing identification.

Facebook's "Groups" and "Marketplace" applications are two of the more well-liked features by college students. "Groups" captures users' tastes and enthusiasm for particular social and cultural activities or predilection for everything from the serious ("Story of a Rape Survivor") to the silly or "Just for Fun" groups (The Flip-Flop Appreciation Society"). Through Groups, members exchange information and if a real-world group exists, members will plan and organize meetings and events through its virtual Facebook Group. Users can browse or search for existing groups to join, or create a group. Creating a new Group with Facebook requires a user to enter a Group Name, a network affiliation, a description of the group, any recent news of the group and contact information for the group founder or officer. Facebook will allow a group's creator to choose access and function options. The group can be discussion board, Wall and photo enabled or not; all related groups can be identified or not. Access to the group is determined by choosing "the group is open" to anyone; "the group is closed" requires administrator permission, or "the group is secret" and will not appear in searches or on the group's member's Profiles. Additionally, a Group can decide to "Publicize" and its name will be shown on the Networks page and in search results. Other users can be invited to join the group by entering the names of Facebook friends or the e-mail addresses of nonusers by utilizing the "Invite People to Join" feature. Groups can be deleted at any time and users can end their membership by clicking the "Leave Group" on the group's profile page. Any action that a member takes on the group page, however, is fed to the News Feed. Facebook's "Marketplace" application facilitates user-to-user sales. Books can be sold or bought on "Marketplace Book Exchange," parking spaces are rented, music performance tickets bought and sold. Users can search the Marketplace or list items to sell or items needed to purchase. Users can post services such as music lessons or tutoring, and post job openings or professional qualifications.

Facebook users are always updated on what their friends are doing on Facebook. The "News Feed" function keeps users informed about such things as what Applications their friends have added, edited, or deleted, what events friends have attended, who has written on a friend's Wall, or changes in a user's relationship status. Users can control these updates by changing their Preferences on the News Feed icon where they can determine whether they want to get fewer or more "Story Types" on News Feed items by clicking "Less About These Friends" or "More About These Friends". The MiniFeed chronicles what the user does on his Profile as well as keeping track of what all his friends are doing. Just as the News Feed can be customized by the user, so can the MiniFeed be modified and tailored to the user's preferences.

Facebook also gives users the option to post a Facebook "status." This is a short open-ended message that users post for their friends to see. The Facebook status has been compared to the "away message" users post on AIM. It is used to share a statement or sentiment. Users can see their friends' Facebook statuses when they sign in. Recently updated statuses are listed on the home page that appears right after logging in, on the same page as the News Feed. When users click on their list of friends, they have the option to see a list of friends Facebook statuses.

What Students Report about Their Facebook Use

We embarked on a multimethod research project to better understand college student online culture through an examination of students' perceptions of their Facebook use. Because the subjects of the study, traditional-aged, residential college students, experience life in both real and virtual communities, it was necessary to employ a methodology for our study that would allow the researchers to capture elements of both of these worlds. In a sense, due to the rise of popularity of social networking sites like Facebook, and computer-mediated communication in general, contemporary, residential colleges function as "hybrid environments" (Ruhleder, 2000) where the real and virtual interact and overlap. In these spaces, face-to-face encounters blend together with online activities. This requires researchers to seek out new ways of studying technological activity (Ruhleder, 2000). With this in mind, our study was primarily ethnographic in nature, as it examined the Facebook campus culture.

Three primary data collection tools were utilized in our examination of students' perceptions of Facebook and online campus culture, two investigative surveys, and a series of ethnographic interviews from which we build the student portraits in this chapter. A questionnaire to explore and situate the ethnographic interviews was administered in the fall of 2006 to students at a large, private institution who had Facebook accounts. Students were invited to participate in the online survey through an invitation posted on the Facebook site, displayed only to members of the institution's "network." A total of 123 respondents answered the open- and closed-ended questions. The responses to the survey were coded and used as the basis for the second investigative survey, which was administered in the fall of 2007. The sample for this questionnaire included 20 colleges, public and private in the United States. Many of these institutions had a history of their populations being active on Facebook. Students were again invited to participate through invitations posted through their Facebook "network" and more participants were generated through snowball sampling. Three hundred and twenty-one undergraduate students at residential institutions responded to this second survey. The first questionnaire was open coded, and then axially coded, until three dominant themes emerged from the data. The second questionnaire was based on these three themes. Then the data from the second questionnaire were coded, using the original codes from the first questionnaire as well as new codes that emerged. The results of the survey were coded and used as the foundation for questions in the ethnographic interviews.

In recent years, the scope of ethnographic methodology has evolved and expanded to make room for the study of online environments (Markham, 2005). Most of this research has focused on communities that exist exclusively online. One of the main limitations to this research is that it requires a more deliberate exchange of information because the researcher and participant are not in the same physical space. In addition, this work is complicated by the researcher's role in the online field (Markham, 2002). In our interviews, because of the hybridity of the participants' community, we merged the concept of traditional research (where researcher and participant are both present) with the direct observation of the online environment, in this case, participants' Facebook accounts. During the ethnographic interviews, we asked participants to open their Facebook profiles, and to explain the content and respond to questions about what we observed. This way, we could ask participants to interpret and make meaning of what we were observing. A total of 20 undergraduate college students were interviewed, from a variety of residential institutions. It is also important to mention that as ethnographers, we also did some general observation of random Facebook profiles and online culture. The interview data were coded using both the codes from the two exploratory surveys as well as new codes that emerged. Through this constant comparative approach (Creswell, 2007) we were able to saturate the primary thematic categories.

From the initial questionnaire, three dominant, interrelated themes emerged from 126 initial codes and 37 collapsed codes that informed the second broader sample questionnaire. These themes were (1) agency, (2) performance, and (3) relationality. Within each of these themes, it was evident that student use of Facebook was governed by the degree to which students felt that they controlled self-presentation (agency); how they believed that they can regulate the presentation of "self" online (performance); and the broadening and reconfiguration of campus community and the consequent growth in student online interdependency (relationality). These three themes were tested in the second questionnaire and other items were also added to reflect the three emergent themes, and to explore secondary themes such as Facebook use as procrastination, addiction, and the differences in use based on gender, race, and SES identities. The second questionnaire confirmed the salience of the primary themes and added depth and complexity to the construction of the ethnographic interview.

The ethnographic interviews generated many conclusions and observations. For example, students made it clear that their Facebook use is mediated by their racial and ethnic and gender identities. Students' agency and performance of self in the virtual environment as marked by race/ethnicity and gender was evident in both the students' testimonies of their decision-making processes regarding use, self-presentation, and impression management, as well as in students' posted images. For example, students of color often talked about being very mindful of displaying images that would undermine their academic credibility on campus. Students of color were very aware of the differences between their profile constructions and those of White students. On the other hand, White students were generally unaware of race/ethnicity distinctions in self-presentation. Student participants generally acknowledged that women are the more active users; that is, women take and upload more photographs and attend to online self-presentation more so than men on campus. This latter observation was especially salient among both sets of questionnaire respondents.

In each of the questionnaires, the term *stalking* was prevalent. In the ethnographic interviews, students explained stalking as largely an innocent voyeuristic and information-getting process, though some acknowledged that unacceptable, obsessive stalking behavior did occur. Though stalking emerged as secondary in the relationality theme, in the interviews it proved an invaluable gateway to understanding how students use the social networking power of Facebook.

The interviews and questionnaires underscored Facebook as the choice online social networking site among residential college students who claim ownership of Facebook because it was designed for their niche community and their social needs. Interviewees use Facebook as a quasi-campus center in which and through which they schedule events, parties, and disseminate campus news. It is also the primary means of online communication between students (e-mail is not for peer-to-peer communication) and serves as the main directory for students. Student leader testimonies describe a heightened consciousness about self-presentation and impression management, not unlike that of students of color. Lastly, there appears to be a developmental curve that characterizes Facebook use among participants. Testimonies suggested that the meaning and culture of Facebook use in the first two years of college life is developmentally specific. The purposes and patterns of use had evolved for juniors and seniors suggesting that the meaning and assertion of online agency, performance, and relationality had changed for our student participants.

Student Portraits: Kris, Jordan, Teresa, Matthew

We present here four student portraits framed by the four central themes that emerged from our surveys and ethnographic interviews. Students' perceptions of Facebook and online campus culture are encapsulated under broad but consistent themes that capture their observations about online campus culture, their awareness of their use, how their identities factor in their consumption, and how they understand themselves as voyeurs and producers of their own representation. We have categorized these themes as "Use-consciousness," "Campus Culture," "Identity Factors," and "Voyeurism and Impression Management."

Kris

Kris is a senior at a women's college in the Northeast majoring in health sciences. An honors student, Kris is involved in a number of campus leadership activities. She is a resident advisor (RA) and secretary of her campus's gay, lesbian, bisexual and transgender (GLBT) student group. She is a member of the rugby team, and up until this year, she was a member of the soccer team, which she gave up to make more time for her academic commitments. She has also been a tour guide and has participated in a number of community service activities including an Alternative Spring Break Trip. Her hometown is a suburban area in the Northeast. Kris is White and identifies as a lesbian. She began using Facebook during her first year at college.

Use-Consciousness

Kris's current profile picture features her posing, arms outstretched and grinning, with a Disney character, a photo that was taken on a recent family visit to Disney World. Kris says that she generally chooses photos for her main profile picture that show her "goofy" side. In addition to revealing an aspect of her personality, however, in order for a picture to be displayed it is imperative that Kris approve of what she looks like in the photo. "I always look for one that is good and goofy and represents me in a way," she says. When Kris has had the same profile picture up for a while, she will look for a new one to swap it with.

As a student leader, Kris has a high level of consciousness about her own use of Facebook, as well as insight into how other students use Facebook for self-expression. Kris says that her role as a student leader, especially an RA, influences the way that she uses Facebook to connect with others as well as her impression management. For example, Kris puts her contact information directly on her Facebook page so that her residents can get in touch with her. Kris says that a lot of students use Facebook in this way—that it has replaced online or paper directories on campus; when students are looking to get in touch with one another, whether it is through Facebook or by phone, e-mail, or Instant Messenger, they turn to each other's Facebook profiles. This use of Facebook as the primary campus directory was supported by the other undergraduate Facebook users to whom we spoke. Kris also employs Facebook to communicate with her residents about floor activities and programs that she organizes for them.

Kris's role as a student leader also influences her impression management. For example, although she is friends with her residents on Facebook, she does not allow them to see the same information on her profile as others who are her Facebook friends. Kris's residents see her limited profile—they can't see Kris's pictures or Kris's wall. Kris says that this is because she doesn't have enough control over what pictures friends will tag her in or what messages they will write on her wall. In other words, Kris will only let her residents, other students for whom she is expected to uphold community policies and standards, see the content on her profile that she directly controls. Kris views part of her role as a student leader as educating others how to use Facebook and manage their own profiles in terms of the images that they portray. Not only does Kris's role as an RA dictate how others will interact with her on Facebook, it plays a role in how she interacts with others. Kris controls what information others can learn about her through her profile, but she also limits what information she learns about others. For example, Kris says that she tries not to look at the profiles or pictures of her residents because she doesn't "want to find anything." "I just don't want to deal with that," she says.

Kris has a high level of consciousness about her impression management on Facebook, but this doesn't mean that she is free from negotiating the boundaries between the different roles she plays on campus. As a student leader, she has to constantly navigate between the multiple selves she presents to different campus audiences. When she was under the age of 21, Kris said that she did engage in underage drinking, a behavior she was conscious about publicly portraying because of her roles as both RA and student athlete. Now that she is 21, Kris still does not like to post photos that show her drinking because she says that it is unclear when the photos were taken and therefore others might assume she is underage in the photos. Kris notes,

> ...everyone is like, yes, but you're 21 now. And I'm like that is correct; I am but, one, who knows when these pictures were taken? Like they could have been, you know, a year ago. And, two, [it could look like I'm] drinking a lot. I don't often do it, and I often will go to parties and not drink. And I still take goofy, crazy pictures with everyone who is drunk. And so everyone just assumes that I'm drunk.

Kris says that photos can misrepresent one's identity—a statement supported by others in our study. Photos are often authentic, but perceived by students to be misrepresentative because photos overplay one aspect of students' selves and neglect to show others. Usually, this is the case if the photos are taken at parties, the occasion when the students in our study told us most photos are taken. Photos are taken less frequently in other arenas of campus life, which also represent students. For example, no students showed us photos of them studying in the library or working at their campus jobs. And as Kris says, photos taken at parties are judged by the context. They may give the impression that a student is a frequent partier, when he or she may only drink occasionally, or photos may appear to show varying levels of intoxication, which may not be accurate.

Kris talked about a time when she felt she lost control over which identity she portrayed to different audiences. Kris usually reminds her friends of her leadership position on campus and asks them not to tag photos of her drinking on Facebook because they are linked to her Facebook profile. According to Kris, one student posted a photo of Kris drinking and tagged her in it. "She is not one of my closest friends, so I don't think she gets it," Kris said. The photo showed Kris performing a keg stand. According to Kris, her face was not visible in the photo. However, the picture was taken at a costume party, and Kris had decided to dress as a soccer player, attending the party wearing her soccer uniform. Therefore, although one could not see Kris's face, her jersey with her number was visible, identifying her to anyone familiar with her identity as a soccer player.

Kris immediately untagged herself in the photo, so that others looking at her profile could not see the picture. However, one of Kris's residents approached her about the picture about a month after it was taken, informing Kris that the resident had seen it. Even though Kris has taken the photo down, the student who originally posted the photo had not removed it from her own profile. Therefore because Kris's resident was Facebook friends with the student who posted the photo, the resident could see the image. This caused a dilemma for Kris. Should she approach the student who had posted the photo and ask her to take it down or tighten her security settings? Kris recalls:

> So I definitely thought about it for a while; and I was like you know what? I decided not to do anything; because I wasn't tagged in it. And the only reason that this girl knew it was me because I was wearing [my number] on my back.

In retrospect, Kris says she realizes attending a party wearing her soccer jersey may not have been a good choice, but she also acknowledges the difficulty in managing the consequences of this choice. Even though Kris untagged or detagged the photo, it still remained posted on another student's profile. This limited the control Kris felt she had over her impression management, something she takes seriously and works hard at. In general for students like Kris, with a high level of consciousness and knowledge about how to control information, impression management in the online social world proves difficult.

Campus Culture

Kris describes Facebook as a central part of campus culture. If one is not a member of the online campus community, she is missing out on an essential aspect of campus life. According to Kris, there is a consciousness about Facebook that pervades social life. When students are at a gathering, they take photos of one another with the premise that these will later be posted on Facebook. According to Kris, she has been at parties where, after a photo is taken, she hears others occasionally asking the photographer not to post the image online. Although Kris accepts Facebook's centrality to her own school's campus life, she was surprised to learn of its ubiquity, the role it plays among college students nationwide, and even internationally.

> People are like...this is an awesome picture. This is going to be my Facebook picture or like this is such a Facebook picture. It's definitely a fact...I heard people when I was somewhere away... in another country or another setting or something. And someone was like this is going to be a great Facebook picture. And I was like, oh, my God, like that is crazy, you know, it's everywhere.

The pull of Facebook is so strong, that many students refer to it as an addiction. It has an addictive quality because of the pleasure it provides its users but also because of the sense of dependency it creates. In her junior year, Kris decided to give up Facebook for Lent. She had a hard time knowing that conversation could be occurring online over which she had no control. During her hiatus from Facebook, someone started a group about her—a sort of fan club—knowing that she could not view the group. When she returned to Facebook after Lent was over, Kris found that the group had over 90 members who had been posting comments to the group's wall, some of whom Kris knew and some whom she never met, including accepted students planning to attend Kris's college the following year. Some comments were directly related to Kris and others were not. For example, someone posted a message encouraging others to lobby for equal rights to gay marriage. "I don't mind. I think it is kind of comical," Kris said, "But, I mean, I'm not an ad for gay marriage."

For Kris, Facebook has been a major part of her campus culture. She talks about a developmental shift in her use over her time in college, a trend we observed from speaking with other students as well. As a senior, Kris is in the position to look back and reflect on her use over time. She says that her use "peaked" during her sophomore year and that she uses Facebook much less frequently now, mostly just checking when she has a new message or wall post. There has also been a shift in her communication on Facebook. At the beginning of college, she spent a lot of time interacting with friends from home, and now she spends more time interacting with friends from campus. Kris has also begun to envision her use after college and has been pondering the role that Facebook will play in her professional life.

Identity Factors

Kris's sexuality plays out on Facebook. According to Kris, she does not list her relationship status, or the sex of the people she is interested in on her profile because she believes that everyone who needs to know about her sexual orientation already does:

> I am interested in women. And I at first didn't put that, because I didn't want people to find out [on] Facebook before I told them. And now everyone I want to know knows...so why does it matter?

The question of whether to "come out" and reveal one's sexuality on Facebook was a choice each gay, lesbian, and bisexual student we interviewed had considered. Kris is in a relationship with another woman on campus. However, she says that she chooses not to list this relationship publicly (by listing "in a relationship with" on her profile), because she does not want this information public in case she and her girl friend ever break up. Kris had a boyfriend in high school, and when this relationship ended, Kris had to remove the text in her profile which listed her relationship status. Kris said this public declaration of her break-up was "horribly awkward." According to Kris, listing who one is in a relationship with on Facebook isn't really necessary because "most people can figure it out from the pictures anyway."

Voyeurism and Impression Management

Kris talked to us about stalking—a behavior that was a theme in our conversation with students and that will also be discussed in the other student portraits. According to Kris, she once stalked her ex-boyfriend on Facebook, learning information about him and his interactions with others that she wouldn't normally have access to. Since her ex-boyfriend went to another college, Kris asked a friend who went to that same college if Kris could use the friend's Facebook username and password to access that college's network. Although Kris's profile is visible only to those who she requests or accepts as friends, some students allow everyone in their campus network to view their profile. Signing into Facebook under that name of someone in another network would allow Kris to have access to anyone's profile that was open to the network. After Kris and her boyfriend broke up, she entered his college network in order to learn more about some of the girls he was spending time with. Kris claims she was not jealous, but she was curious about what these girls looked like and what they had posted on their profiles. She acknowledges that she could have gotten some of this same information from asking a friend that went to the same college as her ex-boyfriend. Instead, she was able to gain this information quickly and anonymously.

Jordan

Jordan is a heterosexual male who attends a large university in an urban area in the Northeast. Jordan considers himself to be biracial/ ethnic; half Colombian, half Anglo-American. Jordan grew up in suburban New York State, is a sophomore, a math education major, and an aspiring teacher. According to Jordan, he is involved in a number of activities on campus, including student government and a few different mentoring programs. He enjoys skate boarding, sports, and video games. Jordan started using Facebook during the summer before he started college.

Use-Consciousness

Jordan says his profile picture was taken by a female friend at a party when he was at home over the winter break. Although no alcohol appears in the photo, Jordan, who is 19, claims that he was drinking that night. In the picture, he is smiling subtly at the camera, his hair in a Mohawk style, which at the time the photo was taken, was a recent update to his look. In fact, Jordan says that this is his first profile picture that features him with the Mohawk. Shot in black and white, the picture is somewhat artistic in nature. Jordan says he chose this particular picture because he liked the way he looked in it—he liked his smile and the way his eyes look in the photo. He claims that when he is smiling in photos, he does not usually like the way his eyes look. Jordan says that he does not generally take photos like this photo—most photos that appear on his profile page have been taken by others. In the original photo, he was featured with a female friend, but he has cropped the photo so only his likeness appears.

Jordan likes to exaggerate how he presents himself on Facebook, primarily to be funny. He will often play with his Facebook status, a one-line message, posting a statement about himself that is either exaggerated or not true. He enjoys putting up "stupid stuff" to see how his friends will react, either through his Facebook status or in the information he lists about himself on his profile. For example, he is a Republican, but says he is rather moderate. Under political views on his Facebook page, he has listed "very conservative."

> When I first came to school, my hobbies [listed on Facebook] were going to church and voting Republican…the only reason I did that is like because I was coming to a liberal school. And I just wanted to be that guy.

Even though the content of Jordan's profile may not represent him literally and may contain information that he admits is exaggerated or untrue, his profile is still a direct reflection of his identity because it shows him as a playful guy who likes to joke around with others. Jordan says that he exaggerates other details about himself, not necessarily to be playful, but because Facebook will allow him to change subtle details about himself without others necessarily knowing about it. For example, Jordan has changed his height on Facebook. He claims that he is actually 5'10" although his Facebook profile lists him as 5'11".

Jordan's profile can be viewed only by his friends. He says that while some people add friends automatically, he is more cautious and won't accept friend requests from people he doesn't know. He doesn't have his home address listed on Facebook, but he does have his school address and he is wary about who can view this information. Jordan says that overall, the information he displays in his profile is only meant to give whomever is looking at it a glimpse of his personality, but to learn more about him they will really have to get to know him.

For the most part, Jordan considers himself to be uncensored on Facebook—he rarely untags photos of himself that are posted online by others. He engages in underage drinking and does not take down photos of himself drinking alcohol when they are posted by others. He says that he does not care about censoring these photos and representing himself in this way.

I don't think it is a big deal. You know I think that it is more like a political issue than a Facebook issue. I think that the reason drinking is such
a problem and even drugs are such a problem is because like the United
States makes it such a big deal. I really think it is a big political thing
like, because like if you go to Europe, people in Europe drink socially.
Like, they don't drink to get drunk...if you go to Europe, like when
I go to parties on my Mom's side where there are like Spanish people
from Colombia, they're drinking socially. Like, no one gets drunk...so
I don't care.

Besides his feeling that drinking should be socially acceptable, Jordan says that he does not mind posting pictures of himself at parties
because this behavior does represent one of his identities. "I present
myself like a party guy. I like to go to parties. I like to be out."

The image that Jordan presents on Facebook contrasts with the one
that Kris chooses to show. Both engage in active impression management, but each has different levels of comfort with the behavior they
portray as part of their identity on Facebook. Although he does have
many "party pictures" visible on his profile, Jordan does say that the
photos that are taken of him are not as revealing as photos that some
other men have posted on their profiles. According to Jordan, both
women and men, but especially men, post nude photos of themselves.
Nothing explicit is visible, but it is implied that they are nude. Jordan
says that he posted one photo of himself with his shirt off, but that in
general, he does not post these types of photos.

Like Kris, Jordan says that the photos that are posted on Facebook
can misrepresent one's identity, which is frustrating. "Pictures give the
wrong impression." For example, he claims that some photos make
him look like he has been drinking when he has not. In other photos,
the context is easily misinterpreted by the viewer.

There is this one picture of these two girls kissing. I'm in the background...I really didn't want people to see that, because like it was sort
of weird like...[I was] cheering them on. [But] that's not what I was
doing. That is what the picture looked like.

Jordan doesn't feel that he has a lot of control over his self-presentation
on Facebook because of the way photos can be misrepresentative.

Jordan also thinks one of the problems with Facebook and impression management is that most students don't understand how to correctly use their privacy settings. When one first signs up for Facebook, his profile is open to his network and he has to change the settings in order for the profile to be visible only to friends.

> So there's so much stuff that you don't realize people could see when you first sign up... people can find me automatically no big deal, but they can't look at my profile. But [when you haven't changed the privacy settings] people can find you. They can look at your profile. They can look at your pictures. They can do everything, just like MySpace. And people don't realize that.

Jordan learned that his profile was open to his networks when a young woman who he was not friends with on Facebook made a comment to him about something displayed on his page. He then learned how to adjust the privacy settings and tightened controls on who could view his profile.

For Jordan, one audience that has access to his profile, but which he cannot always control, is his family. Jordan's older brother is on Facebook and lives at home with Jordan's parents. Occasionally when photos of Jordan are on Facebook, his older brother will show the photos to Jordan's parents. Jordan says that his parents have seen photos of him drinking on Facebook, which they were angry about. Jordan said that he was nervous because he planned to go to a party that weekend and knew that photos would be taken and posted on Facebook. Jordan recently pierced his ear and has a feeling that his parents will learn about his new look through Facebook, when his brother shows the photos to them. He thought his parents will disapprove and be mad at him for piercing his ear. It was through Facebook that his parents first viewed his Mohawk hairstyle.

Campus Culture

While Jordan's older brother, who went to a community college, is on Facebook, his younger brother, who is in high school, does not have a Facebook account and primarily uses MySpace. According to the students we interviewed, this was a generally accepted division among users. High school students and those who did not go to college use

MySpace and those who attend or attended college use Facebook. For example, Mario, a student from Texas has a lot of friends from home that did not go to college. He communicates with them primarily through MySpace while he uses Facebook to interact with peers at his urban college in the Northeast. When asked what he would do if he could no longer use Facebook, Mario said that he could take it or leave it. But when faced with the thought of being disconnected from MySpace, Mario said that would pose a problem for him; he would lose his lifeline back home to his friends who had not gone to college. Jordan, like most college Facebook users, prefers that Facebook stay exclusively for college students—that high school students stay on MySpace until they are ready to make the transition to postsecondary education.

Jordan enjoys using Facebook for social networking on campus. He says that Facebook helps him to stay in touch with people he has met on campus, especially in the college of education. It makes him feel more confident about knowing others at a large school. "It makes me feel like I have 145 friends here." Jordan likes that when he walks down the street in the city where his school is located, he will recognize people. Jordan says that he has not used Facebook to meet people per se by looking through profiles. Rather, it helps him to keep track of the people he has already met. When he wants to communicate with these new friends, he will just send them a quick message on Facebook, instead of an e-mail. Like the other students in the study, Jordan said that Facebook was the primary way to communicate between students, replacing e-mail. Our students reported that they use e-mail to communicate with faculty or administrators, or for other formal communication.

While Jordan enjoys the social aspect of Facebook's networking, one of his criticisms of Facebook is that it no longer has an easy way to network with classmates. As part of the Facebook platform, there was a function where one could list one's classes and easily connect with others in those classes, a feature which Jordan says he misses being able to use. (We later learned from another student that there actually is such an application where one indicates classes on one's profile, but it is now marketed by an outside distributor, and the application has to be downloaded to one's profile.)

However, Jordan is concerned that using Facebook may be replac-

ing some face-to-face interaction between students. This may not necessarily occur in the sense that students are communicating with one
another online instead of face to face. But, according to Jordan, sometimes students will spend time together looking at Facebook rather
than interacting with one another.

> I'll have a friend come over and he'll come over and check his Face-
> book...if he has a message [in his inbox] or somewhere on his Wall
> or something...Hey, I thought we were hanging out, but you want to
> check your Facebook—right. I think it's just another thing that is going
> to be on people's minds.

What about being friends on Facebook with administrators or
faculty? What role do administrators play in students' online social
world? Jordan says that there is a dean at his school with whom he is
friends on Facebook. According to Jordan, he knows for a fact that
this administrator attempts to friend "all guys who join a fraternity."
Jordan was pledging a fraternity at one point, although he decided
against pursuing his membership. Although, according to Jordan,
the dean attempts to friend students who join groups or post events
related to the fraternity, Jordan actually met the dean and became
friends with him during orientation. He thought the dean was a cool
guy and didn't think it was a big deal to be his friend on Facebook at
the time. According to Jordan, professors, on the other hand, should
not be on Facebook because they are not part of campus social life.

Using Facebook to procrastinate when one is supposed to be doing
school work was a theme that we have frequently heard about from
students. Jordan regularly uses Facebook to procrastinate, especially
through using the various applications on his profile. Jordan has over
20 applications—more than any other student who showed us his or
her profile. He refers to these applications as "time killers." Jordan
says that his procrastination is usually unintentional—he will go on
Facebook when he is bored, and find himself looking through the
photos of people he is friends with.

Like Kris, Jordan has thought about the future of his Facebook
page after college graduation: "So like apparently when I go get a job
as a teacher, I'm supposed to untag all the pictures of me drinking and
stuff like that." When asked where this message came from, Jordan

said that he heard it from older students that he works with at a local elementary school. The message about public accountability for Facebook is passed down not through school or administrative authority, but through those who dictate the culture of Facebook—college students themselves.

Identity Factors

Jordan talked about how he perceived differences in Facebook use between men and women. He told us "the girls at parties" had taken most of the photos on his Facebook profile page and that women took more photos in general than men. While there were close to 400 photos of Jordan linked to his Facebook profile, he said that he had only taken about nine photos. In fact, Jordan doesn't even own a camera:

> If guys take a picture, it's usually like if something very funny happens, like it's on their mobile cell phone. So the girls are the ones with the cameras. My Mom was going to get me a camera for Christmas. But I was like no, I'm never going to use it.... Girls have like their purses and they can put [cameras] right in there. But guys, we don't have any room in [our] pockets for a camera.

When we asked other students about this assertion, that women took most of the photos on Facebook, more than men, they told us it was true. For example, Steph, a student at a large institution in the Northeast said:

> I rarely see boys taking pictures, and you know, you don't really see guys at the parties, or wherever you are at, saying things like, "Oh, I wanted to get a picture right now. I should have brought my camera." I actually don't hear that.

Not only do women take more photos than men, however, there also appears to be differences in the types of photos that men and women take. The nine photos that Jordan had taken mostly featured his family, whereas women's pictures most often featured themselves with or without friends and often posing for the camera. Men's photographs often featured travel destinations.

In terms of racial and ethnic identity, Jordan says that Facebook allows him to express this aspect about himself. Jordan displays his ethnic identity primarily through some of the applications that he adds to his Facebook profile. Being able to express his heritage is particularly important to Jordan who considers himself to be bicultural. Facebook allows him the opportunity to post a specific identity, so, he believes, people do not have to "guess" his racial or ethnic identity. Students can be very specific about their ethnic identity, for example, saying that they are Puerto Rican, Dominican, or Colombian rather than simply, "I'm Latino."

In terms of Jordan's sexuality on Facebook, he too is conscious of how he displays this. He doesn't choose to list his relationship status, but he also chooses not to list who he is interested in. According to Jordan, he doesn't want to list "anything I can get" because he is "not that type of guy". Here, again, we see that indicating relationship status is a unique alchemy of college culture.

Voyeurism and Impression Management

Jordan also talked about the act of stalking. He says that college women tend to engage in stalking behavior more frequently than college men. According to Jordan, his ex-girl friend use to stalk him when they were dating. She would continually click on his list of friends to see who he had recently added—and if he had added any attractive women. She would look at who posted messages on his wall, and who was featured in the photos in which he was tagged. Basically, any aspect of Facebook she could check, she would. According to Jordan, "my ex-girlfriend stalked me the whole time [we were together] when I was in college." Jordan dated his ex-girlfriend during his first year of college, when she was still in high school.

Do men also engage in stalking behavior? According to Jordan, they do. He thinks that "jealous guys" stalk the most, and he admits to looking at his ex-girlfriend's wall to see what posts are written on it. He says that in order to be considered stalking, the behavior has to be categorized as obsessive. When someone checks another's person's profile every day (like his ex-girlfriend did to him), that's stalking. According to Jordan, there is a difference between stalking someone and just looking at their photos, catching a glimpse into their lives.

Teresa

Teresa is junior at a large institution in the Northeast. She is from Boston and identifies herself as Haitian and Argentinean. She claims that no one would know she was Argentinean just by looking at her. Teresa is an art history major and aspires to go to law school to become an attorney. Teresa is involved in a number of campus organizations, among them the Latino student organization, and the Future Black Lawyers Association. Teresa joined Facebook the summer before her first year of college when she was participating in a summer transition program at the college. Teresa is heterosexual and is dating a sophomore football player on campus. The football program at Teresa's college is Division I with a fairly high national profile.

Use-Consciousness

Teresa's Facebook profile picture shows her at a formal ball she recently attended. Dressed up in a gown, she is posing for the camera with her boyfriend Jon, a tall, attractive Black male. Although Teresa and Jon have been dating for almost a year, Teresa says that this is actually the first photo she has used as her profile picture that features him. In the past, she has been hesitant to post a "couple" photo. Teresa decided to post this particular picture because she wanted to post the image of the ball without having to make an entire photo album, and she thought she looked good in the picture. "We have been going out for so long. I don't have to be like shy about it anymore."

Teresa says that she changes her profile picture frequently. Recent profile pictures she has posted include a photo of her with her girlfriends on New Year's Eve and a photo of her with her father and three brothers. Like the other students we've portrayed so far, Teresa says that she definitely has to look good in a picture for her to feature it as the main photo on her profile page. Teresa is not as playful with her profile as Jordan, but she will occasionally use Facebook to play a joke or have fun. For example, at one point, Teresa used a photo of her sister, who looks very much like Teresa, as her profile picture in order to see if any of Teresa's friends would notice the difference between them.

According to Teresa, she checks Facebook "all the time." Her use has increased since she got a Blackberry wireless handheld device. She has a program, Facebook for Blackberry that sends her a text message whenever she has received communication through Facebook—if someone has posted on her wall, sent her a message, or commented on a photo of her. She can also access Facebook from her wireless device because of its Internet capabilities. Facebook already sends users e-mail messages alerting them to new communication via Facebook. Therefore, some students use e-mail to learn about messages on Facebook. If Facebook is the primary medium for student-to-student communication, the function of e-mail becomes to reroute students back to this arena. Some students, however, do not like to be notified of updates from Facebook via e-mail and have these messages sent to noncampus e-mail addresses that they rarely use.

Teresa is very conscious about the photos that are posted of her on Facebook. This consciousness extends beyond untagging and detagging unflattering photos, however. Teresa knows that when photos are taken, they will likely appear on Facebook. Therefore, she poses and tries to look her best at the time that the photo is actually taken. Teresa also does not like to be photographed with alcohol if she has been drinking and takes precautions so that this does not happen.

> I'm posed, and…if I drink that night, I don't want them to be on Facebook the next day. You know, like [at a party people say] this is going on Facebook, and then you move, you know. You don't want to be in it. I usually don't try to get photographed that much and…I mean…there's a lot more pictures of me, I am sure, but I actually untagged a whole bunch of them.

Teresa says she is slightly less concerned about being photographed with alcohol now that she is 21 years old, but she still likes to exercise a lot of control over which images of her are both captured and portrayed. In fact, as she shows us her profile, she untags photos of herself while she is talking about them, saying that she does not like the way she looks. Teresa has already considered the role of future employers on Facebook. "I know that a lot of employers like to look at Facebook, and I am very aware of that, and I don't want them thinking that I am a train wreck." Her awareness of this had already played out in her impression management in contrast to both Kris and Jordan who considered editing one's profile for an employer was something to be considered later.

For the most part, Teresa must know or have met the people that she is friends with on Facebook. She said that recently, she has been going through her Facebook profile and unfriending those people whom she does not talk to that often. Teresa explained a little bit about the politics of unfriending someone.

> [There is] this boy who used to have a crush on me, and I wouldn't talk to him, so he unfriended me, then friended me back on Facebook, then unfriended me again, then friended me again…. It is like a back and forth. [When someone unfriends me] I am looking at pictures and, all of a sudden, I can't click on your name, and I'm like, whoa, I thought we were friends on Facebook. So, it is a little nerve-wracking.

Although she strives to limit her friends to people she has regular contact with, she says that she is friends with some people "for other motives," like being able to view their profiles. Teresa's friends can see her entire profile, except for one young woman who Teresa says she does not want looking at her albums. Teresa has adjusted her privacy settings so that this young woman can only see Teresa's limited profile.

Like Kris and Jordan, some of Teresa's friends on Facebook are family members. Two of Teresa's siblings, a brother and a sister, are on Facebook. Teresa's brother is also in college and Teresa's sister is a junior in high school. In terms of Teresa's other siblings, Teresa has an older sister who she says is not on Facebook, and two younger brothers, who are "too young" for Facebook. "I hope they don't get Facebook until they are 18," Teresa said. Teresa does not find herself in the same situation as Jordan, with her parents learning about her actions through photos of her that her siblings view on Facebook. Teresa says that in general, she would rather her mother didn't see photos of her drinking, but that if she has something that she really did not want her mother to find out about, she would never put it on Facebook. She also tends to tell her mother information about herself before her mother could learn about it on Facebook, for example, when she started going out with Jon.

Teresa says that her use of Facebook and the way she expresses herself on Facebook has changed over the time that she has been on it. When she was first on Facebook, she was making a lot of new friends and wanted to give a good first impression. Now that, as a junior, she knows more people, Teresa does not feel that she has to reveal as much information and put herself out there as much online. She has changed and deleted information from her profile.

> I used to have a whole bunch of groups, too, and I started erasing them. I started taking them out because it's like, you change…you change what you do on Facebook. I used to have all these things describing me, but I feel like now, whoever [views my profile] knows me by now. I am a junior—whoever knows me already knows me. I don't have to have all these silly descriptions.

Campus Culture

Teresa says that Facebook is fundamentally about college; that high school students don't take Facebook seriously enough. This she knows from her experience with her sister whose judgment about profile content she regularly questions. Teresa, like the other students we talked to would prefer that Facebook be for college students only.

> It is definitely about college…because you get to post your classes, what you are doing, you know, what activities you are [involved in]. If you have a group, if you are part of an organization and you want to get a message out, you send it through Facebook. And, you know, if you want to get in touch, or in contact, with somebody or, you know, say hello, [you can use] Facebook for this, too.

Teresa says that for residential college students, when one connects with another on Facebook, that person is much more accessible than if this exchange occurred between two high school students.

For Teresa, Facebook has been part of her college experience since she moved into her first college residence hall, the summer before college when she attended the summer transition program. According to Teresa, the other participants in the program encouraged her to join. Through being on Facebook the summer before college began, Teresa was able to stay connected with her friends from high school while at the same time orienting herself to campus culture.

I would look for pictures, and if there were any pictures of parties, [I would look at] who is hanging out with who, who are the girls that are like the pretty girls, you know, and like it helped me get a sense of how the social life here is, you know, what happens at parties, how people usually dress.

It was through Facebook, connecting with other students and viewing their photos that Teresa first learned of campus social norms.

Not only did Facebook provide Teresa with a way to communicate with campus classmates, it was also through Facebook that she first started to communicate with Jon. When the two met on campus, Jon asked for Teresa's phone number, and she told him that he could just Facebook her instead. According to Teresa, she told him this because she didn't know him that well and felt that it was too personal to give him her phone number. Jon sent Teresa a message on Facebook the next day—a private message as opposed to a post on her wall. The message said: "I wonder if I am going to get that number, or is it still off limits, or am I going to be regulated to just a screen name, or maybe, if I am lucky, I can have both."

Teresa did give him her phone number and they went on a few dates the following week. Then the next Saturday, Jon asked Teresa to be his girlfriend. The first thing Teresa said, when she agreed, was that they needed to put their relationship status on Facebook, listing each other's names after "in a relationship with." She listed that she was in a relationship with Jon, and Jon confirmed that it was true; then their profiles were linked through their relationship status. Students we talked to had different thoughts about posting relationship status online. According to Teresa, "When it is on Facebook, it is like official, you know? If it is not on Facebook, it is not really official. You [are] not really a couple." Again, the alchemy of campus culture and relationship status is evident in this observation.

Teresa and Jon mostly communicate by phone and text message now, although they will send messages on Facebook. Teresa will also occasionally "poke" Jon. The poke, part nudge, part wink, part flirtatious hello is an interesting feature of life on Facebook. Students used this poking feature in different ways. Some students engage in "poke wars," with one another—returning the poke whenever they sign into

Facebook. Although primarily friendly, poking has even been used for teasing, although in a good humored way. On a bus ride, a student at a New York City college told one of the authors that before large basketball games at her college, students will poke players on the opposing team. Therefore, when the players sign into Facebook, they find that they have hundreds of pokes from students at the school that they are slated to play.

What groups does Teresa belong to on Facebook? Most groups that Teresa is in mimic actual groups she is part of on campus, like the Latino student group and the Future Black Lawyers Association. She is also a member of groups representing events, such as the Miss Collegiate Haiti pageant that is held every year at her school. Like Kris, Teresa even has a "fan club" group on Facebook that a friend started about her. There are all different types of groups on Facebook. One type of group that is powerful, and which has an effect on campus culture is the "In Memoriam" group. When students pass away, other students will often form a group to remember that person by posting photos and writing on the group's wall. Teresa is a member of a group dedicated to a classmate who died. When she visits the group's page and looks at the wall posts she is surprised by the first post that she sees. "That was from yesterday. Wow. She died a year ago."

Identity Factors

In terms of gender, Teresa supported the conclusion that women take many more of the photos on Facebook than men do. "Girls are obsessed with photos." She says that Jon will ask her to take photos of him at football games so that he can post them on Facebook. She says that he actually has many more pictures on his profile than she does, but that none of them were actually taken by him. "He doesn't really take pictures, not at all. He doesn't, no. He had a camera and it broke, and he never fixed it."

Teresa says that for the most part, she and Jon have the same types of pictures posted to their profiles—pictures of them at parties or with friends. But Jon also has a lot of pictures posted of him playing football, and almost always has a football image as his main profile picture. After the recent ball, Teresa asked Jon if he would change his profile picture, and post one of the two of them at the ball, as she had, but he didn't want to do this. He told her he just wanted to keep his football picture up. Teresa says that guys have a fear of appearing "cheesy."

In terms of her racial ethnic identity, Teresa says that she used to feature this on her profile, in the form of an application where one can display one's heritage through posting flags on one's Facebook profile—the same application that Jordan uses on his profile. She used to post both the Argentinean and Haitian flags on her profile. She also used to include reference to her ethnic identity in the About Me section of her profile. However, she has more recently decided not to include these as part of her profile. She said that it became a hassle to change her About Me, and that, in terms of the flags, she grew annoyed with having too many applications on her page. "At first I thought it was cool to have my flags there, but then I was like...who cares?" At some point, Teresa said she felt expressing her ethnic identity on Facebook became unnecessary. "Everybody who knows me knows I am Spanish."

Teresa had a lot to say about and the differences in Facebook use she perceived between of students of color and White students. This was an area in which the White students we talked to were more limited in their responses. Most White students did not notice a difference between the types of photos posted of students of color and White students. Some White students mentioned that they thought that there likely was a difference in the images posted by members of different racial and ethnic groups, but they couldn't point to what that difference was. According to Teresa, being conscious of one's image before photos are taken—rather than after the fact—is not just a characteristic of her use, but also distinctive of many students of color, who seem to be more conscious of their impression management in general. "Students of color, if they look bad in the picture, they will take it out. They will untag it. They make sure that it is not there."

Teresa says that she generally observes differences in behavior from White students and students of color. Instead of taking measures to avoid being pictured using alcohol, Teresa perceives that White students make efforts to appear with alcohol in photos.

I have a lot of White friends, and they love to take pictures when [they] are messed up, and [they are] looking drunk...they don't care if they look messed up, like they don't care if they look really drunk in a picture, they won't untag it.

Teresa says that although she observes these general differences in patterns of behavior between White students and students of color this is by no means a generalization to apply to all students. There are plenty of students of color who pose with alcohol all around them, or even smoking marijuana. She says it really depends on what individual student one is talking about.

Gabriela, a Black student at a women's college in the Northeast, had similar things to say about the trends she observed on Facebook between students of color and White students. She also talked about students of color in general, and Black students in particular being much more conscious of their impression management. She says that in general, White students will put up more photos featuring alcohol consumption. Black students will post pictures of them partying, maybe dancing, but not necessarily drinking. She says this is not because Black students do not drink; the alcohol is just in the background of the photos they take instead of a central feature.

I definitely think that [Black students are more careful about the photos they post on Facebook.] This is from my experience from some of my friends...there are a lot of faculty on Facebook and I feel that being a student of color, they feel that there is already that and things are against you so...to go out and [post pictures of drinking]...its not a smart thing to do.... They definitely try to be a lot more cautious. So there's wild partying, but you don't see drinking a lot.

Gabriela says that in photos that show drinking, White students are "all tagged," whereas Black students "don't want to tag [themselves] in compromising pictures."

Regarding sexuality, students seem to differ about the information they wish to post on their Facebook profiles. Where some students, like Kris, are hesitant to reveal too much information about their relationship status on Facebook, other students, like Teresa have the sense that a relationship is "not official" unless it is on Facebook.

Teresa does say that although she holds this view, it is not one shared by many men. According to Teresa, males are much more conscious of their relationship status because they don't want to appear "off the market."

Voyeurism and Impression Management

Teresa says that she engages in stalking, or at least assists friends to accomplish this task. According to Teresa, she recently had a friend from another school who wanted to look at the profile of a female student from Teresa's university whose profile was open to others in Teresa's school network. Teresa gave her friend the password to her account so that the friend could view this student's profile. According to Teresa, her friend was looking at the student's photos, but also for other information such as wall posts. What is the reason her friend was seeking this information? The young woman at Teresa's school is best friends with a young woman that Teresa's friend's boyfriend used to date. So, the friend was, in a way, checking up on her boyfriend—seeing if he had any contact with his ex-girl friend's best friends. Since she didn't have a connection that would allow her to access the ex-girl friend's profile, this was the next best thing.

Teresa believes that she does not stalk her boyfriend, but she does keep close track of communication others have with him on Facebook. Teresa says that Jon's self-presentation and identity management on Facebook are different because he is an athlete on a high profile team. He has a different level of consciousness about how he should present himself and who might be looking at his profile. When Teresa checks Jon's profile page, she looks to see if anyone has written on his wall. According to Teresa, Jon gets lots of wall posts, many from "fans" who he does not know personally. Teresa says that it is her responsibility to be "aware of the groupies." If she sees a post that she does not like, she will ask Jon to delete it.

Teresa also monitors her sister's profile, checking regularly what she has posted and teaching her about proper Facebook use.

> I do check what is going on, especially with my little sister. At one time, she had...you know how you have statuses?...she had a ridiculous status, and I was like, you need to take that down, and I told her that that is

not appropriate…and one time she had a picture with a bikini on, as a profile [picture], and I said, "You take that down right now."

In another case, Teresa's sister posted that she was in a relationship with another student from her high school. Teresa didn't think that they were in a relationship, but she friended him "just to make sure it was nothing." Teresa, as a college student, is the one who dictates the proper way to use Facebook to her sister, still in high school, through regularly monitoring and checking her behavior on the site.

Matthew

Matthew is a gay Black male and a sophomore at an urban university in the Northeast. He is originally from Texas. Matthew considers himself politically active in terms of gay rights and he is on the executive board of his school's gay, lesbian, bisexual and transgender (GLBT) student association. He is majoring in romance languages and literature. Matthew joined Facebook fairly early, when he was a junior in high school and taking classes at a college in his home state, which was a requirement at his high school. At that time that Matthew joined Facebook was not yet open for high school students to join, but Matthew was able to get an account because he had a college e-mail address.

Use-Consciousness

Matthew's profile picture shows him reading the newspaper. His head is turned away from the camera and his eyes are focused on the paper that he is reading. The photo was taken at a business conference that he went to in New York. Matthew says that he is "really picky" about the photos that he posts on Facebook to represent himself. He tries to include pictures where he thinks that he looks good, and intellectual, but prefers not to be wearing his glasses. Generally Matthew doesn't make a habit of taking photos for the purpose of putting them on Facebook. Rather, he will go through the pictures he has taken and choose the ones he deems most suitable for his Facebook profile.

Matthew is "out" on Facebook. His profile lists that he is interested in men. According to Matthew, if someone is socially out, it makes sense that someone would list that in his profile. Because, after all, "if someone asks me [if I am gay] I am going to say yes." Matthew says that when someone does not reveal sexuality on Facebook, others usually guess through photos and text that appears on the page. The absence of a posted relationship status on Facebook profiles is also a signal about sexuality, according to Matthew. Some people, Matthew acknowledges, may not be socially out, or they may be out on campus but not back home. This affects how they might portray sexuality on Facebook. For example, Matthew has a friend who has two different Facebook profiles linked to two different e-mail addresses—one profile is for those in her campus community who know she is out and the other profile which is more conservative—the side of her she portrays to friends from home, who do not know about her sexual orientation.

Matthew's Facebook profile is open to everyone in the network at his school, but only his friends can see his photos. In terms of friends, Matthew says that he must actually know someone for him to add them as a friend on Facebook. On the Facebook home page, there is a long list of friend requests waiting for his approval. He says he just ignores these friend requests. Rather than ignoring the requests, he plans to leave them on his page until he can remember who people who friended him are. Matthew says that he feels guilty about hitting the "Ignore" button.

Campus Culture

Like Kris, Jordan, and Teresa, as well as many other students with whom we spoke, Matthew would prefer that Facebook were more exclusive and limited to college students only. For him, Facebook is about college, although he acknowledges that someone in high school might say something different about the purpose of Facebook. For Matthew, one of the reasons that Facebook is tied to college culture is because all of his friends on Facebook are in college. He doesn't have a lot of friends in general who did not go to college. In addition, Facebook has always been about college to Matthew, even when he was in high school. Because Matthew joined Facebook before it was open to high school students, he had the chance to enter the college online social domain early. This experience contrasts with that of Teresa's sister who joined Facebook during a time when many high school students had found their way into this world and were dictating their own culture on Facebook, one that occasionally disagrees with those standards set by the original, college student users.

Not only did Facebook play a role in exposing Matthew to college campus culture when he was a junior in high school, it also oriented him to the college he would be attending during the summer between high school and college. When Matthew and the other students learned of their housing assignments, one of the other students who was going to be living in Matthew's residence hall formed a group and most students slated to live in that hall joined, including Matthew. According to Matthew the students used the group to ask questions and to try to learn more about what living in the residence hall would be like. Matthew also said that since then he has helped orient others to his campus community through Facebook. He has had prospective students in high school contact him through Facebook to ask for his impressions of his university. Matthew returned the student's message, sharing his opinions about the experience he had so far.

Matthew finds Facebook a helpful tool in his day-to-day life as a college student. Like other students, Matthew uses Facebook as the primary campus directory. He says that when he meets a classmate but cannot remember her last name, it is nice to be able to sign into Facebook and locate this information. Matthew also uses Facebook as his primary form of communication with other students. The Facebook message has replaced e-mail as the communication medium of choice for student-to-student contact. Facebook makes communication between students possible if those students do not have each other's phone numbers or another way to get in touch. Matthew said that when a student wanted to know when the next Gay Party, organized by the GLBT student association would be held, he messaged Matthew. The other student knew that Matthew was on the board of this organization, but he did not have Matthew's phone number. Facebook was a quick and easy way to get this information.

As a leader of a student organization, Matthew uses Facebook to communicate with club members, and to advertise campus events held by his organization. He does this by creating an event page and using it to invite others. He also uses his profile picture to advertise events, a behavior we observed from other students as well. Right before an event, Matthew will sometimes change his profile picture to a flyer advertising the event. Matthew says that it is easy to get the message out about campus events because of the way Facebook connects students to one another:

> I think it is easier to network with people...if there is someone you talk to at a party randomly because you have that Facebook connection, then it makes it easier to tell that person there is another party and develop a friendship that way, whereas you might not have before.

Matthew also says that electronic flyers posted on Facebook advertising events may have replaced physical paper flyers posted around campus. In fact, the GLBT student group has been considering discontinuing their use of paper flyers:

> We have been considering not postering because everyone does everything through Facebook now anyway, so it is kind of pointless. No one will pay attention to a flyer, but they will go to Facebook to see basically what is going on.

Other students who spoke to us acknowledged that the paper flyer posting by organizations is dying out on campus and being replaced by Facebook Events. In large urban areas with several colleges and universities, posting events on Facebook is an especially efficient and effective way to get the word out about events. For example, as another student, Mark noted, his African-American fraternity will post meetings on various local networks to increase their participation at events. Students' charity events are also frequently posted on Facebook Events, and predictably, so are college-specific parties. With the Facebook Events application, college and university students can browse campus events or search for specific real-world events. The application allows for "open" events to which all Facebook members have access and can add their own name to the guest list. "Closed" events require an invitation from the event administrator, or the Facebook member who created the event. Users can request an invitation from the event administrator who is the only user who can create the guest list. College and university students also use Facebook to invite specific friends to "secret" events. These events are invitation-only events and are received by Facebook notification or e-mail only to a particular guest list. Alison, a scholarship student at an elite private university, remarked that she often browses campus events on Facebook to see what students are attending which parties; or to see who the "cool" people are and with whom they socialize.

The perception that Facebook has become the social registry on campus was evident across all students with whom we spoke. Whether or not students are habitual or sporadic Facebook users, college and university students recognize that Facebook is a major source of social information on campus. As Kris discovered when she attempted to give Facebook up for Lent, it is not socially accepted to be absent from Facebook because of its centrality to campus culture. However, Matthew told us the opposite was true as well: it is not good to be perceived as using Facebook too frequently.

> I think it is probably not cool to have the perception that you are on Facebook all the time. Even though everyone knows that everyone is on Facebook, and that everyone uses Facebook, it is probably not cool to like have a profile that is like...this person doesn't have anything better to do than talking on Facebook all the time.

Gender and Other Identity Factors

Matthew agreed that women use and post more photos than men, including gay men. Women are more likely to have more photo albums than men. Matthew said that he had a lot of photo albums, but that was because he had been abroad the previous year and had posted photos from his travels. Other students told us that one main difference in males' and females' photos is that when males do post photos, travel is one of the primary content areas featured. In addition to the travel photos Matthew does have a number of photos linked to his profile that were taken at parties. He says, however, that these photos were all taken by women.

In terms of differences in Facebook use between students of different racial backgrounds, Matthew said that he really didn't feel he could comment on that because a difference was not visible to him. He said that although racially exclusive friend groups did exist at his university, the group of friends of which he was a part was heterogeneous and mixed racially. This made it difficult for Matthew to spot any trends between students of color or White students.

Matthew had quite a bit to say about the politics of sexuality on Facebook. Some students choose to list their sexuality on Facebook in the form of the "interested in" field like Matthew, while others, like Kris, choose to leave it off. If one's sexuality is not clear from one's Facebook profile, others will make assumptions about one's sexuality through what they see as clues on that person's Facebook page. For example, Matthew says that if a person lists that he is male, interested in friendship, and does not list "interested in," he is probably gay. Another student said that someone was gay if he did not list his sexual preference, but had "very liberal" listed for political views.

According to Matthew and other students we spoke to, there is a lot of playfulness about sexuality that occurs on Facebook, usually in the form of relationship status. There is clearly a difference between men and women and the degree to which this playfulness is accepted. Matthew says that when two men are listed in a relationship on Facebook, chances are they are most likely actually in a relationship in real life. Men do not joke that they are in a relationship with one another unless it is actually true. On the other hand, it is fairly common for a heterosexual woman to indicate that she is in a relationship with another heterosexual woman. According to Matthew, a woman can be listed in a relationship on Facebook with her female best friend and that's accepted.

According to Alison, a female student who identifies as bisexual, this is one aspect of Facebook culture that angers her:

> It annoys me because you almost never see two guys who are straight in a relationship on Facebook. But there are a lot of girls in relationships and girls kissing girls—that makes it seem that being bisexual or being a lesbian is kind of a joke thing to do. This girl has legions of photos of herself kissing other girls and she's heterosexual. There's something offensive and annoying about that. It's not a joke—it's a real sexuality.

Voyeurism and Impression Management
Like other students we have featured, the object of Facebook stalking has been former romantic relationship, an ex-boyfriend or girl friend.

Matthew said that at one point, he used Facebook to try and figure out who his boyfriend from home was now dating. Once he learned the identity of the new boyfriend, Matthew said that he no longer cared and stopped Facebook stalking his ex-boyfriend. Matthew was satisfied with just that information he was able to access through Facebook. The two men are still Facebook friends, but do not have contact. Recently, Matthew received an event invite to a housewarming party for his ex-boyfriend and his new boyfriend. Matthew looked closely at the invitation, considered the invitation but then moved on.

Matthew says that when he wants to learn more about a person he just met or whom he already knows, he will look him up on Facebook. He said that for example, he had just talked to a guy for the first time in an elevator on campus. He looked through the man's photos, but that was about it. Matthew didn't return to the profile repeatedly. According to Matthew, there is a difference between Facebook stalking and real-world stalking. Facebook stalking is accepted behavior on campus, whereas stalking in real life is taboo. "Facebook stalking is just looking up someone…and looking at all their pictures, but I mean, everyone does that."

Though Matthew believes that he presents himself authentically, like other college Facebook users he does actively manage his online impression. His concern about appearing studious, intellectual, and the "businessman" he aspires to become, affects his decisions about images he posts and his privacy control choices. His albums, as we recall, are not open to all of his friends, and he uses his profile picture to send particular signals or messages. The posed profile picture reading the newspaper with glasses or the photograph used in conjunction with an event invitation are ways in which Matthew, like many other students who participated on our study, manage and direct self-presentation with particular ends in mind. Some African-American women are particular about posing for Facebook pictures dressed in what they deem particularly stylish outfits that they perceive signal not just their fashion sense but a social class position. Diego, a Latino student often changes his profile picture and Wall to show his ethnic identification, even his sports fanaticism. Having varying degrees of concern over the impression presented on Facebook, Matthew and the other students talked about how they manage self-presentation in ways that reflect both their self-consciousness as individuals and as young women and young men with particular sociocultural group identification.

Our Observations

Listening to Matthew, Jordan, Teresa, and Kris and the many other students who talked to us about their Facebook use, it was clear to us that among college students the culture of online social networking sites like Facebook has emerged to reflect late-adolescent, undergraduate concerns about their agency especially as it related to identity—how they present themselves and how they manage that presentation. We observed in their commentary much of what the social science research literature profiled earlier in this text has revealed about online culture but did take note of the unique ways in which students use Facebook to craft identity, to shape campus culture, and like all other technologies, to improve communication within and beyond the college campus.

Students assume authenticity on Facebook, believing that though some level of counterfeiting is exhibited on profiles, most profiles are accurate representations of the person. Authenticity appears to be a function of two conditions. First, given Facebook's niche and relatively bounded nature, students seem to take for granted that Facebook users are other community members. The "community" here is some presupposed direct connection to a college or university, whether that connection is immediate (another student) or one that is perceived as being further removed from the primary college campus connection (e.g., high school students, faculty, family). The college students who took us through their Facebook profiles implicitly trust other members, a condition facilitated by students' confidence in the site's bounded nature. Still, college and university students' Facebook consumption is not naive or without critical assessment. Students engage in checks of authenticity very mindfully by further investigating profiles or friends, or shorthand with established campus cultural signals (recall Matthew's observation about relationship status). Interestingly, students accept varying degrees of identity playfulness and ironic representation, a characteristic of their developmental and

generational positions. Our students accepted online identity performances as fluid and in flux and did not judge self-presentations as
disjointed or fragmented despite some developmental psychologists'
concerns (Gergen, 1991). Students spoke about their self-presentation and impression management, and the presentation of others on
Facebook as synchronic—as something they understood was real or
authentic at a specific moment (Kris being goofy; Matthew looking
intellectual) and diachronic—changing over a period of time (Teresa
taking down her flags; Jordan's haircut and ear-piercing).

But all students, whether unambiguously or by intimation, understand their own self-authorship through self-presentation on Facebook as bodied interactions; that is, not as virtual or avatar. Students
perceive their Facebook selves as not the digital personification of
themselves, not the embodiment of the idea of "self," but actually as
self—though still fluid, sometimes satirical, sometimes performative.
Students' authenticity on Facebook is like real-world performances of
gender or race or sexuality, of social class or ethnicity, performances
that reveal cultural narratives of normative and counternormative
behavior. Online campus culture is stimulated by real-world sociocultural narratives of how students should or do behave (Teresa assumes
the conventional feminine role of photographer for her boyfriend; as
an athlete and resident advisor, Kris monitors images in which she can
be perceived to be engaged in inappropriate behavior), as well as coun-
ternarratives that reflect developmental and generational sensibilities
(public identification as a gay man or lesbian). Like Butler's (1990)
translation of the meaning of "drag," college students' self-presentation and impression management is not fully free-play but rather a
demonstration of how individuals desire to be "read" or interpreted.

Generally, relationships made public authenticate our identities and
among our student Facebook users this was certainly true. Facebook
is predicated on this principle—that those with whom we are connected and whom we are "friends" with—associates members with
membership in culturally constructed groups. Facebook members
are associated with students at their college and as such are read as
having some assumed attributes of that campus culture and community. Facebook members, like our students, embody gender, racial,
and ethnic identities that are also communicated online in a myriad

of ways; for example, through photographs, group memberships, and Wall postings. Less clear and requiring more precise reading of tacit cultural signals and cues is how Facebook associations signal identification with social class categorizations. Students we spoke with by and large did not testify that particular postings or Facebook behaviors were clear signals of social or economic class. Instead, we heard students refer to indicators of social or economic class status. For example, students who were first generation college goers were those students who spent more time on MySpace, primarily communicating with friends who did not attend college or who were at institutions closer to home. As mentioned earlier, African-American and Latino/a students seemed particularly concerned with how they would be read by others, especially faculty. Not uncommon among ethnic and racial minority students on predominantly White campuses, the need to be seen or interpreted by racial/ethnic majority students and faculty as legitimate (i.e., not lower class, undeserving students) is evident in those students' Facebook profiles. They appear to take great care to present no opportunity to question their academic and personal claim to college membership; they seem particularly cognizant of the necessity to project socially and culturally "acceptable" representations of self to White students and faculty. Though no student said specifically that Facebook is racialized space like MiGente or BlackPlanet, it does appear that for many of the college students who spoke to us, Facebook allows them to make racially or ethnically relevant associations and to fortify their cultural identities. These students were conscious of the need to steer a course for self-presentation in which the public and private dimensions of race and ethnicity could be effectively managed.

Our students did and didn't challenge real-world cultural norms and did and didn't import these norms into online campus culture through Facebook. It was not clear to us, for example, that men were more expressive and more emotionally open on Facebook despite Lanthier and Windham's (2004) conjecture about gender online. Our survey responses and interviews revealed that women are the more active and proficient users of Facebook, adhering to traditional real-world gender conventions about communication and self-presentation. Women in our study were the photographers, far more likely to spend time customizing their profiles and homepages, more prone to be concerned with standards of beauty, while men generally did not engage in as much detailed profile construction and though they showed interest in how they "looked," the concern was less about conforming to normative beauty and more about individual meaning. Men seemed more explicit about what their self-presentation portrayed—Matthew the intellectual businessman; Jordan the mischievous Mohawk, earpierced independent young man, liberated from his parents' authority. These young men do and don't care what others think of them as a consequence of their online representation; they appear to be more autonomous actors than some of the women. On Facebook, the young men in our study seemed to conform to many of the cultural narratives of masculinity, especially that as young men they are self-determining and self-legislating. Women like Teresa and Kris, for example, spoke about online self-presentation as restricted by social norms genderspecific to women—Teresa making sure that her sister's profile picture was not sexualized in a particular way (pictured wearing a bikini); Kris always taking into account her family, her friends from home, her younger residents, her teammates, and her women's college norms of acceptable student conduct.

As researchers Ellison et al. (2007) observed, students form and maintain social capital online because they stay connected and associated with a community, or in the case of Facebook, many communities within college communities. There is campus communal interaction on Facebook, and that was clear in the responses to our survey and in the tours of students' profiles. The concern that an online campus community would engender introversion or reclusive behavior was not evident in our study, quite the contrary. The view of campus online culture in this study supported Katz and Rice's (2002) assertion that online interactions facilitate sociability and stimulate communal activity. We cannot say whether the students in our study would be less or more social and engaged in campus culture without Facebook, but we do know that their extensive use of Facebook as a social register, as a space in which and through which their sociality is expressed and performed, is vibrant. It is true that most friends on Facebook are not intimate or close in the real world, but it was not clear to us that students used the accrual of Facebook friends as social capital, despite

Marwick's (2005) assertions. However, our students did make judgments about other students based on that person's friends. A user's social graph—her network of associations, her list of friends—can be interpreted as social capital in that it signals to others the user's connections within and between social groups. As social capital, there is implicit value in a student's network of associations because it is in and through these networks that students engage in the culture of the campus and in the ecology of self-development. The value of associations networked is the cornerstone of online social networking sites and given our students' accounts of their Facebook use, college students recognize this and capitalize on it. Whether using the social graph to reinforce real-world relationships or using the social graph to vet new associations or group membership, Facebook is a conduit of social capital on college campuses today.

Note

1. All student names appearing in this text are pseudonyms and their institutional affiliation has also been masked.

4

THE NEW CAMPUS REALITY

Facebook and Student Affairs Practice

The student portraits detailed in chapter 3 reveal the nature of campus life online, a new reality that these students say is central to their college experience. In their own voices, these students share their perceptions of behavioral norms as well as how they think identity is constructed and interpreted in the online social world. How these and other students talk about identity in this context, however, seems to be in opposition to the paradigmatic view that student affairs administrators, those professionals primarily responsible for the oversight of campus life, hold of college student identity. On Facebook, college student identity is distinctly postmodern. Students shift between multiple selves and experiment with different identities, revealing alternate faces to their audiences by taking advantage of the agency they are afforded by Facebook's privacy settings. As Kris, Jordan, Teresa, and Matthew, the students whose stories we told, showed us, they have to constantly navigate between these selves when they post aspects of their identities online. It is not an easy task. Even those like Kris, with a high level of consciousness, rarely do it perfectly.

The postmodern student self is defined outwardly, through relationship—whom one is friends with, whom one is in a relationship with, what groups one belongs to—rather than through an inner reflection. The postmodern self is a dispersed, "fragmented" self that is very much fluid and in flux (Gergen, 1991). At the same time, student affairs administrators seem to view students in a unified way, as the "whole student" (American Council on Education, 1994; Evans, Forney, & Guido-DiBrito, 1998). As students have moved more and more of their social lives online, administrators have continued to attempt to understand their development through a modernist lens.

This has led to a cultural mismatch. Is that student in the photo doing a "keg stand" in her soccer jersey really Kris, the responsible RA, the diligent student? How could it be? But yes, it really is Kris. All of those identities belong to her, though she does not understand them to be fragmented or disjointed.

But online social communities of college students can no longer be simply student space. To college and university students, these communities are real, extending from and intertwining with their day-to-day lives on traditional college campuses. Campus culture now includes the online campus. In order to effectively reach college students, student affairs administrators need to recognize, understand, and accept this new campus reality. They must come to understand what it means to do their work in this hybrid culture where the real and online interact and overlap and face-to-face encounters blend together with online activities. Student affairs administrators must now directly deal with online relationality as a copresence with face-to-face association. If behavior is a function of the interaction of the person with environment (Evans et al., 1998; Lewin, 1936), how is this complicated when the environment is a hybrid one that includes both real and online elements?

This chapter will help to explain the role of student affairs administrators in the context of campus life online. We will apply the conclusions voiced by students to the different administrative areas of campus life, from admissions to alumni relations, in order to explain how best to work with college students in the new social world. We will highlight positive aspects of online social networking sites and how administrators can benefit from understanding them. Though we recognize that administrators have focused on the negative or problematic aspects of Facebook culture and behavior, our objective here is to present student affairs practitioners with possibilities for appropriating the productive power of online social networking for college student development and growth.

Do Administrators Belong on Facebook?

As the students in both the interviews and survey results told us, there is a commonly accepted value that Facebook is about college, and many wish it were exclusively for college students. As Facebook continues to broaden its audience and more users from outside of college become part of the community, this wish for exclusivity has only become stronger. Currently, over half of all Facebook users are outside of college, yet college students still continue to cherish Facebook as their own. This means that student affairs administrators, although very close to the center of campus life, are still on the periphery of the online social world at the colleges where they work. Administrators can open profile accounts on Facebook, peruse groups, and even accept student requests to become friends, but students don't really consider administrators to be members of their online niche community.

According to the students we talked to there were mixed feelings about the role of administrators on Facebook. Alison, one of the students whom we interviewed, said that she had heard administrators ponder recruiting students to attend her college through Facebook and she thought that was "creepy." There was also a misperception among students about the role these administrators wished to play on Facebook. Students talked about administrators searching for inappropriate and illicit student behavior on Facebook. There emerged a sentiment that administrators' authority translated into a desire to seek out infractions to discipline students. For example, Jordan talked about the dean whom he believed friended every male on campus who was joining a fraternity, so that he could keep these students' activities under surveillance.

One student, Steph, expressed concern that having administrators as part of the online social community would fundamentally alter the online campus culture. "I feel it is just kind of like Big Brother looking in otherwise, and, I don't know…Facebook would be a very different culture if…faculty and administrators were on basically." Steph also said that she believes there are faculty and staff who are lurking on Facebook, signing on with profiles that are not visible, to check up on students. "I feel like that is invasive." Steph did say, however, that she might make an exception for an administrator who was young or a recent college grad because he or she could speak the language of Facebook and understand online campus culture.

Some of the students who said that they were friends with administrators and welcomed their presence on Facebook were most often students who felt that they "had nothing to hide," or they were student leaders who were very conscious of impression management. Some students were friends with administrators, but only allowed these administrators to see their limited profile. They blocked certain aspects of the profile from administrator view, such as their photos, or the wall. Even though students seemed to feel that generally administrators are alien on Facebook, they appear to feel even more strongly that faculty members do not belong in this online space. We explore the role of faculty on Facebook more in the next chapter.

What are administrators to do about their position in relation to the campus life that exists online? On the real college campus, their authority is well known. But what is their role in the online campus? Do they have any authority? Are they welcome? If they are perceived as not belonging on Facebook, how can they educate students about identity development, impression management, and Facebook use? How can we assist students in negotiating the boundaries of their fluid identities? In the online social world of residential, undergraduate college students, student affairs administrators must use caution and be mindful that online campus culture is essentially shaped and managed by college students with their particular sociocultural needs and desires in mind.

Administrators' boundaries on Facebook and their role in the online social world are really not all that different from their position in the real world of college student culture. Administrators are both insiders and outsiders in relation to student life. On one hand they are privy to the inner workings of campus culture, working to promote community and support individual students. On the other hand, they are not quite a part of college student culture because they are not students—and it is the students who ultimately dictate both what the culture is and who belongs in it. Administrators need to be mindful of this ambiguous boundary and understand the nature of their insider/outsider position.

Examples of these two roles play out in the everyday work of the student affairs administrator. For instance, an assistant director of student activities might work closely with the Black student organization to plan a dance on campus, and she might even be present at the dance. But she is not out there on the dance floor. Rather, she's working the coat check, or responding to administrative difficulties or emergency situations that arise. In another case, a director of residence life may be the one to establish a policy for quiet hours in the residence halls during final exams. But at 3 a.m., when a resident is playing her music just a little too loudly, it is not the director of residence life who comes to knock on her door. It is more likely another student or the student resident advisor.

So should administrators be on Facebook? We believe that it's acceptable for administrators to join the online community, but also we don't consider it imperative that they do so. If administrators are going to be friends with students on Facebook, however, we recommend that administrators let students initiate the friend request. If administrators are to be on Facebook, and allow students to access their profiles, however, it is important to think about their own impression management. Consciousness of impression management is especially important for younger administrators who are recent college graduates. Because Facebook has been available since 2004, there is now a cohort of administrators who established their Facebook profiles featuring their undergraduate student identity, rather than their professional identity as institutional authorities. One suggestion for new professionals is to limit their profile settings, restricting access to the students they are friends with, effectively blocking content and images that they do not wish students to see. Administrators could also establish a separate profile page using an alternate noncollege or university e-mail address. Impression management is a topic that should be featured in training sessions and conferences for graduate students and new professionals sponsored by student affairs organizations.

Student Leaders as Cultural Translators

On Facebook, there are students who both create and uphold campus community standards, holding their peers accountable for their online expression and behavior. For example, Kris questioned her residents to consider the role of Facebook and how they expressed and represented themselves online. Teresa taught her little sister in high school about the standards of online campus culture by teaching her what was appropriate to post on Facebook and what was not—asking her to change material when she violated any of the culture's spoken or unspoken rules. When the message reached Jordan about cleaning up his profile page for potential employers, it was sent by older students at his school.

Administrators should pay attention to campus life online and play a role in educating students to manage their self-presentation in this context, but given their insider/outsider role in relation to the community, they should do so with caution. The best way for student affairs administrators to connect with students and dialogue about their Facebook use is through student leaders who are conduits of the campus social world. Student leaders are gatekeepers of campus culture who can serve as cultural translators, bringing the language of online campus culture to student affairs administrators and disseminating educative messages about self-presentation and impression management to students.

Some students we talked to have a high level of consciousness about their self-presentation and impression management on Facebook, taking full advantage of the control they have over profile content and its access. Others, however, showed a naiveté when it came to privacy settings. Jordan, for example, said that he did not know that his profile was open to all members of the Boston network until his sophomore year. In addition, some students do not concern themselves with profile privacy settings because they perceive Facebook to be "safe." This was a sentiment supported by many of the students who completed our surveys. Also, some students don't even discover that their profiles are open unless there is a consequence, like someone Jordan was not friends with commenting on a photo he had posted on his profile page, or Becca, who said that she started getting messages from a "creepy" guy in the Boston network that she had never met or even seen before. As we've said before, to college students, Facebook is about college, and this contributes to the false sense of security that many have regarding their privacy and online use. Many students must learn to strike a balance between disclosure and privacy.

Administrators, through student leaders such as sports' team captains, orientation leaders, and resident advisors, can educate students and raise their consciousness about the level of control that they can have over their profile, if they choose to exercise it. As peers, student leaders are well-equipped to have conversations with other students about their Facebook use. However, student leaders are often compromised because they must shift between their multiple identifications as students like all others and unlike all others; they are and are not peers. Consequently, training for student leaders is necessary to teach them to be a resource for other students about Facebook. In addition, student leader training can educate them about impression management as campus leaders.

Who should conduct training for student leaders? Student affairs administrators who are well-aware of Facebook and campus culture can conduct these trainings. Administrators can conduct these trainings with other students or by themselves. It is important to have a student voice present at the training sessions because it is students that are the true authorities on Facebook, but the administrator sets the tone and answers questions about institutional policy. Our hope is that by reading this book, administrators will gain an understanding about how students construct their identities on Facebook so that they are equipped to conduct trainings on this issue, either with student leaders or with other staff members.

Training for student leaders would give them a chance to discuss their own impression management and reflect on their roles as student leaders online. It would also include reactive elements. Students want to know what the process is when they come across a concerning image or message on Facebook. What does the administration expect them to do? Do the student leaders report the incident immediately to a superior or confront the student themselves? What types of behavior on Facebook should student leaders be concerned about? For example, what are the different possible responses to a photo in which an underage student is having a glass of wine at what appears to be an off-campus party or a Facebook status message that could potentially indicate that a student is suicidal? Student leaders need to fully grasp their roles as gatekeepers of student culture. They need to understand where the boundary lies between enforcing social norms themselves, bringing a situation from online into the real world, and bringing it to an administrator's attention. Conducted and sponsored by the student affairs or dean of students office, training to educate resident assistants (RAs) and other student leaders on Facebook and campus culture is now inevitable.

One of the authors conducted Facebook training sessions with undergraduate resident assistants in her role as a resident director. The training module consisted of three main parts. During the first section, the facilitator talked about how the RAs' roles in the community extended online; the facilitator encouraged students to think about impression management and the inconsistencies between how they represented themselves to their residents on campus and how they represented themselves online. The facilitator also reminded students that the Facebook community was an extension of the real world community and that students were leaders in both campus worlds, impressing upon them the importance of acting on online behavior that concerns them, in the same way that they would enforce behavior that they witnessed in the residence hall or elsewhere on campus.

The second part of the training encouraged RAs to reflect upon the impact that Facebook has upon their campus community. As a small group, students brainstormed negative and positive effects that Facebook could have on their residence hall and greater campus communities. They talked about how to educate students in order to prevent the negative effects and how best to take advantage of the positive effects. Finally, the group discussed how to use Facebook to build community, including using the features of Facebook which make it easy to communicate with a large group of people at once and invite others to events. The training concluded with RAs casually sharing stories about their successes and struggles with their own and others' impression management on Facebook. After the training, one piece of feedback that some of the student participants provided was that they wished to have a tutorial on how to use the privacy settings on Facebook. They understood conceptually the importance of impression management, but they were still unsure about how to carry out the process. They suggested we set up a computer and projector and then guide them step-by-step.

Orientation leaders are another group of student leaders who should receive training on Facebook and online campus culture. These are students who work closely with first-year students during their initial days on campus. For example, at New York University, a session about Facebook is included in orientation leaders' mandatory training. In addition, Facebook is discussed in other workshops on health and wellness and student professionalism. These orientation leaders, in turn, teach a workshop on Facebook to incoming students during New Student Orientation (Hersh & Hinkle, 2007).

Athletes are student leaders that may require special training. It is particularly important to educate athletes about impression management because they are public figures on and off campus. As Teresa mentioned, because her boyfriend Jon is a football player on a high profile team, others who know him only by this identity will look at his profile. As representatives of their school, athletes need a chance to reflect upon their impression management in their role as athletes. At the same time, they also need to hear about consequences for behavior displayed on Facebook and learn about the athletic department's policies regarding enforcement of behavior displayed online. Again, the most powerful message about the norms for self-representation on Facebook comes from a peer educator—another student. Therefore other athletes, like captains or students on an athletic council may be the best candidates to train other athletes. Becca, a student-athlete we spoke to, who is on her college's swim team, told us that she would be intimidated if the athletic director talked to her about her use of Facebook—she would feel defensive and believe that she was getting in trouble because she perceives the athletic director as an outsider to Facebook culture. On the other hand, Becca said that she would be receptive to guidance from her team captain who was her peer.

Orienting Students to Campus Culture, both Real and Online

Orientation to life at college is beginning earlier and earlier. Some of students' first glimpses of institutional culture occur online—for example, through college admission websites and computer mediated communication with current college students. A few students in our study spoke of receiving unsolicited communication from prospective students looking to learn more about the college that they currently attend. According to Miguel, one student we talked to, he had met a few students from the track team on their visit to campus and they followed up with him on Facebook. This was an easy way to stay connected to the college and learn more about campus culture, something that he does not think they necessarily would have done if it weren't for Facebook.

> I think Facebook made it easier. Just because I know they didn't have my phone number. So it was easier for them to just look me up, add me as a friend. I would accept just because you know, I would know them and I would understand why they would do it through Facebook because they didn't have my number or anything like that or they didn't have the chance to talk to me while they were visiting the school.

Facebook allows students to network with peers before even setting foot on campus. Most of the students we spoke to mentioned that they had activated their Facebook accounts before they arrived at college. A quick search of Facebook reveals hundreds of groups dedicated to the class of students who entered college this fall. In these groups, formed by the first students to accept their college admissions offers, new classmates interact with one another—posting messages to the group's wall and message board. In many of these groups, the dialogue between students is unmediated or unregulated—some incoming students post questions and others answer; the students make meaning of the college experience at their institution without administrative guidance.

Many of the students with whom we spoke indicated that they spent time on Facebook in the summer before they attended college, networking with others. Once they arrived on campus, they had the sense that they already knew some of their classmates. For example, one student, Crystal, told us

> It just made me feel so much better coming to orientation and coming to school. I was like, at the very least, I can see someone and say, "Oh, we are friends on Facebook. How are you?" And at least have that.

A couple of students, Matthew and Alison, both told us that they joined groups that were formed by students who would be living in their residence halls and were able to learn more about and connect with the people with whom they would be living.

Student affairs administrators are typically poised to welcome students and to orient new students to the college campus when they move in, or for commuter students, when they matriculate. But students are orienting themselves to campus much earlier online, especially on Facebook. This is likely to help with college adjustment. Administrators should be aware and work with orientation leaders and other student leaders to understand the ways in which students may have already been oriented to campus culture before they actually arrive on campus.

Some of the forums of prospective and new students online are unregulated. Administrators don't need to be on these message boards themselves, but there should be student leaders on the message boards helping to correct misinformation that circulates and also to help these new students negotiate campus culture online. After all they are still in high school and may not have been exposed to the college student standards of conduct on Facebook. During the academic year before college, admissions officers should make sure that there is a well-trained student presence on these sites, such as a tour guide or admissions student worker.

During the summer, students, for the most part, have a clearer idea of where they will attend college and use the online forums for networking with future classmates. These too, should be visited by current college students who can answer questions and help inform incoming students of norms and standards. The banter on these boards is actually quite significant. As students post messages about classes, roommates, and what to bring to school, they are engaging in "anticipatory socialization," trying on the roles of college students and imagining what their life at college will be like. Engaging in "anticipatory socialization" is linked to college student persistence (Attinasi, 1989).

When students do arrive on campus, even though many of them will have used Facebook during high school and the summer between high school and college, some will not yet have figured out social norms of online social networking or as we mentioned earlier, simply be lacking basic knowledge about limiting and controlling the information that is portrayed through privacy settings, about achieving a balance between privacy and disclosure. As part of the college orientation process, administrators should oversee students teaching other students to adjust these settings and engage in active impression management. An orientation could be dedicated to this topic and students could teach others how to use the privacy settings. The discussion about Facebook at orientation should not be limited to its own forum, however. Since it is such a dominant force in campus life, it should be featured as a subject in sessions on other topics, such as alcohol use, sexual harassment, or diversity.

In addition to the orientation process, another broad implication for campus administrators is that Facebook has shifted communication patterns between students. As the students we spoke with told us, Facebook is now the primary vehicle for student-to-student communication as well the first place that students turn for campus directory information. This shift in communication has played a strong role in students' ability to advertise campus events and organize students into groups. Students who are involved in campus organizations tell us that Facebook is now the primary method that they use to inform other students of campus activities. College and university students have found success in advertising this way. Typically students will create an event page and invite Facebook users to attend, or students will create a group on Facebook, invite people to join, and then message members of the group with important information. Steph has used both of these methods for getting the word out regarding activities in which she is involved. For example, Steph is a member of an a capella singing group on her campus. The group creates Facebook events for all of their concerts and invites people to attend this way. According to Steph, she will even invite students from off campus, or friends from home, whom she knows cannot attend, in order to let them know that the concert is occurring even if they can't be there.

Steph has also used a Facebook group for advertising. Steph is a senior and is currently the chair of her Senior Class Gift committee. The committee's goal is to get 50% of the class to donate. She plans to use a Facebook group to invite members of the senior class and then inform them of different events sponsored by the committee. Steph says that she believes this has been a successful way to reach her classmates.

> People would be much more likely to check an event and see what is going on, or join a group, and then see what events the group is hosting than to open up random e-mails from people because a lot of people

get spam e-mail and get tired of it, but people still think that Facebook things are valid, when there is stuff going on, on campus, so they are more likely to read what is actually going on, and that is a new thing this year. I think that the Annual Fund has just started realizing how much of a tool Facebook could be for just attracting attention to something.

Because Facebook is privileged over e-mail as a form of communication, students tend to take the messages that they get through Facebook more seriously. Another student, Diego, also commented on why he thought using Facebook was a successful way to advertise events.

> I think it is a lot better way of communication. I think it is because I think for the most part everyone usually checks Facebook...I think what really increases the number of people that will attend an event is that they post it on Facebook than word of mouth or through flyers.

Students enjoy and have come to expect to receive information about goings on through Facebook. As one student mentioned, she felt that she would not have been informed about residence hall meetings or events if it were not for Facebook.

In addition to providing students with the capacity to spread the word about events and activities to countless people, the multimedia nature of Facebook also allows students to display images of their activities and events online. For example, one student we talked to, Miguel, is a member of an all-male step team at his university. Members regularly post videos of their performances online and then tag each other in the videos so that the videos link to members' profiles. Through these posts, students have an alternate way to let others know about events, retrospectively—they can post photos or videos following an event.

Because Facebook has the capacity for students to network with other students beyond their campuses, it has allowed students to advertise events more broadly. One population that has taken advantage of this has been students of color. In an urban area, students at different schools can network with one another. For example, the Boston Black Students Association has close to 1,500 members. Gabriela told us that she has been able to meet other Black students in the area through Facebook as well as learn of cultural events and parties in the area she would not have otherwise known about. Gabriela says that she has met a number of other Black students in the area at events advertised on Facebook. Then, after she and the other students have met they "[become] closer through Facebook." For example, "this girl we met really briefly through a concert, but then we added each other on Facebook. You can say it's that Facebook made us closer."

In addition, while the real campus is local, the virtual campus is global. Because they use Facebook as a primary method of communication, college and university students post information about themselves and continue to interact with peers, staying connected when they transfer to another institution, take a semester off, or are studying abroad. Students told us that Facebook was a way to share their experiences with students on their home campus and to stay connected to campus goings-on when studying abroad.

Because of these positive aspects of Facebook communication, administrators should encourage the students with whom they work to take advantage of communicating in this way. In addition, students have come to expect communication through Facebook. At the same time, however, when advising students about how to advertise events or send a message to a large group of people, it is important to remember that not every undergraduate student is on Facebook. Yes, it is extremely popular and use is widespread, but membership is not mandatory, so sending important messages that all students must hear is not a good idea. Communication via Facebook can remind or reinforce, but it should not be the only source of communication for students. Remember how hard it was for Kris when she gave up Facebook for Lent? If important communications are sent only through Facebook, students will feel as if there is no choice but to be online.

Supporting Student Development in the Expanding Campus Community

In this chapter we have highlighted the positive aspects of online social networking on the college campus community, but what about the negative aspects? What are the effects when students violate campus policies through the images and text that they post online? What should the consequences be for these actions? Administrators should feel free to react to concerning behavior that comes to their attention on Facebook. Since students interpret what's online as "real," they should understand why there may well be consequences for certain actions. What students seem to struggle with, however, is not the behavior's incompatibility with campus policy. Instead, many students are concerned with how the image was brought to the attention of administrators in the first place. In our professional experience, and supported by students in our study, this incredulity is likely traced back to students' naïveté around privacy settings and the illusion that Facebook is a sanctuary for students free from administrative scrutiny. The ideas we discussed earlier about how to proactively address impression management are intended to prevent these types of incidents from occurring.

Since Facebook intersects with college student identity development, there are implications and topics to consider for administrators on campus who support certain student populations. For those who work with women's centers, one question is how students express gender identity online. Administrators of multicultural affairs may want to think about students of color and their construction of racial and ethnic identity online, as they support these students in their identity development. Those who work with college students broadly will also want to keep in mind that Facebook is a central force in campus life. All administrators working with students, including counseling center personnel, must remember that the online and real are inextricably linked and that students' experiences play out online and vice versa. For example, we heard a great deal from students about the anxiety they experienced over their "relationship status." A student's emotional state may also be complicated by the fact that she changed her relationship status on Facebook, revealing her break-up to all of her Facebook friends. Because it is expressed online, there may be additional consequences. The public nature of such disclosure among college students in late adolescence may have harmful effects.

Parents are another campus constituent with whom student affairs administrators work. The students in our study talked about how their parents were able to learn about the aspects of their lives that are on Facebook, without necessarily even having a Facebook account. In

Jordan's case, his parents learned about his new look (the Mohawk) when his brother showed their parents photos of him that had been posted on Facebook. And in Becca's case, her father, a police officer in her town, saw photos of her drinking alcohol when not yet 21. Someone from her high school also saw the photos on Facebook on Becca's open profile.

How should administrators respond to concerns from parents about Facebook? If parents understand student development, they can assist student affairs administrators in educating their children in a meaningful, appropriate way (Wartman & Savage, 2008). Proactively educating parents about student culture on Facebook will help them be able to support developmental goals. Some services provided to parents by parent relations and other student affairs offices attempt to teach parents about student culture. Since Facebook is now such a major part of campus culture parents should learn about Facebook at parent orientation, through parent newsletters, or other college communications. Administrators could provide parents with an overview of Facebook functions and how it is used by students.

As students transition away from the real campus after graduation they stay connected to the online campus. The time that students spend on the online social campus is longer in duration than the time that they spend on their bricks and mortar campus. Once alumni, students use Facebook to connect to former classmates, network with others, and to remain connected to their alma mater—and even faculty. Alumni relations staff members have begun to utilize Facebook to locate alumni in order to invite them to various events. Homecoming, annual fundraisers, alumni job networking events, athletic events, and alumni mentor and internship programs now populate many college and university alumni Facebook pages. Online campus culture has already extended itself beyond graduation.

From prospective students to alumni, campus life on line holds many implications for administrators. The students' voices presented here are meant to help administrators understand the culture that is campus life online—the new campus reality.

5

THE FUTURE OF THE CAMPUS SOCIAL GRAPH

What Is the Future of Online Social Networking on Campus?

As is the case with all technology, the future of online social networking on college campuses is occurring right now. Changing demographics of social networking sites indicate that older, out-of-college users are increasing in numbers, that global expansion of social networking sites like Facebook has created a multilingual, multinational social graph, and that niche user communities have multiplied. On campus, faculty, college administrators, advancement and alumni officers, campus security forces, employer recruiters, and parent associations are new but active and growing online social networking communities. Off campus, college alumni now use social networking sites like Facebook to connect both in professional and personal respects. More and more, employers use social networking sites as a head-hunting strategy for professional job candidates.

In this concluding chapter, we mull over the impact of these emergent nonstudent communities and contemplate the future of online networking sites on campus. How will imminent and future applications impact the social graph, relationships, and community building among college students? Will these new communities have an effect on college and university online social networking practice and culture? What will matter to the impending Web 2.0 generations of college students already sharing information and networking online?

The Changing Demographic of Facebook and Other Online
Social Networks

In February 2008, the PEW Internet and American Life Project
noted that 92% of adults ages 18 to 29, and 85% of adults ages 30
to 49 were Internet users. Almost three-quarters of adults ages 50
to 64 are Internet users and 37% of those over 65 years old are also
active Internet users. But the telling statistical trend since May 2007
is the dramatic rise in the number of adults over 25 years of age who
have registered on Facebook at a time when the lowest rate of growth
was experienced in the college-age demographic, ages 18 to 24 (Pew,
2008). From May 2006 to May 2007, the most dramatic growth in
Facebook registrations occurred among 25- to 34-year-olds (+181%),
with precollege teenager site registrants experiencing a 149% growth.
A manifestation of Facebook's decision in September 2006 to open
registration to users outside of college networks, these data suggest
that user growth will likely cause the site's demographic composition
to be similar to the whole of the Internet using population (ComScore,
2008). Younger users will enroll in college already social network literate, and college and university alumni—recently graduated or years
beyond commencement—will represent a larger and larger share of
the user community. Social networking sites like Facebook know now
that their fastest growing demographic are users 35 years or older. At
the end of 2007, 48% of Facebook's users were over 25 years old; 53%
of MySpace users were over 25; 35% of Hi5 users were over 25; and
predictably, among LinkedIn users (the business-oriented social networking site used primarily for professional networking) almost 90%
of users are over 25 years old (McManus, 2007).

The expansion of niche social networking sites like Facebook has
raised the issue of where a social media niche can support multiple
smaller niche communities within the larger community. Facebook's
original target niche was the college and university student, particularly the student residing on campus. But since its launch, the site
has extended its reach to high schools, businesses, and now any user.
Becoming more like MySpace, which has no narrow market niche,
establishing a Facebook profile *today* simply requires that the user be
13 years of age or older and, if under 18 years of age, be enrolled in

high school and have a valid e-mail address. It is no longer a condition of membership that users have a college network address. A Code
of Conduct on the site reinforces its original college niche user ethics around authenticity and privacy, harmful and harassing behavior
or content, sharing other users' privacy data, uploading unsolicited
items that are spam, junk mail, or commercial sham, and engaging in
or encouraging criminal activity on the site. However, harassing and
cyberbullying behavior by high school students has been carried out
on Facebook (de Vise, 2008).

Though concerns about how Facebook is used by younger users are
contradictory in some ways to its stated ethics of conduct, the inevitable aging of the teenage population of users seems less troubling for
current college student Facebook users, perhaps because teens' predictable rise as a college-going demographic makes them less incongruent
with the site's niche characteristics. Teenagers, though developmentally a rung below the late-adolescence of the college-going population, are still sociologically comparable to 18- to 24-year-old college
students. Teenagers' online social needs are similar to those of college students. High school students want to stay up to date with their
friends' status; they plan activities online; they are "social searchers"
who investigate other users with whom they have a real-life connection (Lampe, Ellison, & Steinfeld, 2006), and also like college students, they perceive their Facebook community to correspond to their
existing real-life social relationships at school (current classmates or
those who have graduated and gone off to college) or friends from
camp, religious groups, and other institutional affiliations (sports
teams, music groups, etc.). Though perhaps not a user community
that engages in "social browsing" to connect with other users offline
(Lampe et al., 2006), the high school user seems less alien and disparate to Facebook's traditional and original niche user than the older
adult user.

Perceived as "creepy," the older adult user presents Facebook's college
niche community with a seemingly incongruent trespasser. Thus the
"graying" of the online social networking population presents concerns
about the ability of Facebook to maintain its collegiate identity and
function. Preserving their generational and campus Facebook niche
is a growing concern expressed by students in the research presented

in this book, and is echoed by students elsewhere as well. A University of Michigan undergraduate noted that older users "undermine the ties between Facebook and the college community" (Schwartz, 2007, p. 6). Why are older users perceived as online campus gatecrashers? Does older user participation in social media like Facebook undercut a student cultural core?

Recent data on Facebook suggest that "older" users are actually much like current college student users; that is, they are college-educated, mainly White, and the majority is female (Li, 2007). Though adult users certainly don't use social networking sites to monitor and participate in residential campus culture, like college and university users they are social browsers as well as social searchers. Older adult users use Facebook to learn more about people they already know, and to find friends and relatives with whom they want to reconnect. Older adults also use social networking sites like Facebook to locate people or groups with whom they want to connect offline. Adult users stay updated on their friends', coworkers', and extended family's activities, events, and celebrations. New parents post babies' milestones and share their parental travails. Adults use Facebook groups to find volunteer opportunities, to post calls for political and social action, upload photographs of vacations and all other manner of activity, and plan real or virtual reunions of high school friends and college classmates. Graduate students and teaching assistants use Facebook to communicate with undergraduate students in their classes, and to network and collaborate with other graduate students. Professional use among older users seems focused largely on getting to know more about coworkers, and engaging in job networking and professional development; some use Facebook to conduct their work in nonprofit arenas. Overall, older Facebook users appear to utilize the site in much the same way as colleges students do—as a social utility that connects them with friends and others. Like college students, older Facebook users keep up with friends and family, upload photos, share information through text and hyperlinks, and are motivated to learn more about the people they know. Like college students, older users recognize the value of Facebook's privacy settings and controls.

But typically, older users are not traditional residential college or university students; only 12% of Facebook's older users are full-time students. Older users have already lived the college experience and most have moved beyond their campus quads. They are likely to be executives, professionals, work in sales, education, or in the technical fields, and 12% have children 16 years of age or younger (Li, 2007). Developmentally, older users have knowledge, experience, and expertise beyond those of younger college students, yet the central characteristics of online social networking on Facebook are still relevant to their real lives. As one observer of adult use and researcher of social media noted, "people our age are going to find uses for the tool that have to do with the maintenance of life already in process, rather than making one up out of whole cloth" (as cited in Schwartz, 2007, pp. 2, 3). These uses, though by definition congruous with those of the college-going user community, are developmentally distinct, and though to date no research studies have been conducted to assess these distinctions, platform developers and advertisers are beginning to take note of this demographic's unique use. If older users are using Facebook primarily to update friends and family on their own life events—children's activities and accomplishments, their own professional moves and achievements, travel adventures, and political and community activity, then it stands to reason that they are a bounded online community simply overlapping the original community. Yet, undergraduates understand that Facebook is their online social network and assume that the purity of the site as a college and university virtual social medium has been compromised by the intrusion of parents, administrators, faculty and other adults. To the undergraduate Facebook user, the adult world has infiltrated student space, perhaps changing online culture or minimally altering how they perceive the bounds of their online social community. In other words, college students recognize that it's not just campus student friends and peers at other campuses that are on their virtual campus anymore. Consequently, the bounded distinction of the online community—college and university 18- to 24-year-olds primarily living on residential campuses—has faded.

Almost two years after opening the site beyond college and university networks, Facebook put in place new privacy controls that in many ways address some of the concerns that younger college users have about the intrusion of adult users. In March 2008 Facebook upgraded its privacy control features to allow for further and more distinct privacy selections, effectively giving users greater and greater power to manage—generally and specifically—profile access. The main updates included a "standardized privacy interface across the site and new privacy options" (Facebook Press Release, 2008b). With these enhanced privacy options, users can further customize their profile viewing control, fine-tuning who gets to see what on their profiles. The new "Friends of Friends" privacy option allows people to share information only with people they are connected to through their friends. Users now have the ability to share and restrict information based on specific friends or friend lists. Through the "Friends of Friends" privacy option, college users, for example, can restrict access or share information with specific Facebook friends or their friends list. Choosing what information to share and with whom to share it can rebind the college user community by effectively shutting out older users like parents, faculty, administrators, and potential employers. College student users can better safeguard and maintain their online campus culture by using new and more precise privacy settings to block intrusions from user communities with whom they have logical real-world relationships and overlapping characteristics but who are not fully compatible. Despite being linked through a real and virtual social graph, with more precise privacy capabilities, college students can sustain a discernable Facebook sanctuary. Since the central purpose of online social networks like Facebook is to connect real-world associations in a virtual space, and for that matter, to disconnect from real-world relations as well, it appears that updates to privacy settings and improved user consent can further facilitate college users and non-college-going adult users to coexist on Facebook.

Having common characteristics and coinciding objectives, non-college-going adult users and college undergraduate users certainly can coexist within the same online social graph and successfully utilize an online social networking site like Facebook. Ironically, the upgrading of privacy settings is very attractive to adult users also, especially given concerns about employer, government, and advertiser surveillance. Today's college students as a generation weaned on the Internet appear to be predisposed to a conceptualization of privacy that is in some ways different from the traditional or older adult's privacy model. Researchers and journalists have observed that this generation of college student users assumes that privacy is a matter of exercising control over sharing and hiding personal information, whereas older generations believe their privacy to be absolute and categorical (Auchard, 2007; Melber, 2008). Corroborating this observation, boyd (2008) asserts that understanding information as private is for Internet generations a matter of managing self-exposure and stranger intrusion and to what degree they can direct online impression management. College student online social network users in our study certainly say they value "privacy" and use privacy functions in their profiles, but like many of their generation, they still provide highly personal information on Facebook (Acquisti & Gross, 2006). Prior to the new, more detailed privacy settings adopted by Facebook, researchers found that individuals' concerns about privacy weakly predicted Facebook membership and that users disclosed a great deal of personal information despite these concerns. College-going users in this study trust their ability to control their information and its access, and yet appear to know very little about the extent to which their private information is actually disseminated. But for older, nonstudent Facebook users, Acquisti and Gross (2006) discovered that concerns about privacy really only prevent the nonundergraduate population from joining Facebook. User age, as a strong predictor of membership, seems also to characterize attitudes about online privacy and disclosure.

The concern over privacy and what it constitutes on Facebook was brought into relief when the site's News Feed and Mini-Feed features were inaugurated in September 2006, and then again in November 2007 when Facebook launched its "social advertising" program, Beacon. News Feed was intended to circulate and broadcast any newly posted information on user profile pages to all friends in the user's many networks. Reminiscent of journalistic "live" newsworthy event updates, the time-stamped news feed transmitted up-to-date changes of user profiles—what groups were joined, what applications were added, when profile pictures were changed, and other updates—effectively bringing attention to users' personal information to more and more people. Mini-Feed keeps a log of similar events on the user's profile page. Soon after the launch of the applications, users formed a

Facebook group, "Students Against Facebook News Feed" to protest the news feed function and its group membership eventually reached over 740,000 members. Through the group, users protested the News Feed and Mini-Feed, asserting that these functions violated their privacy because their profile information was no longer in their control. User complaints prompted Facebook developers to update privacy settings to allow users to choose what kind of information could be transmitted on Mini-Feed and friends' News Feeds. In an open letter, Facebook founder Mark Zuckerberg assured users that new settings would also identify for users the type of actions they take but that these actions would not be disseminated to other users (Zuckerberg, 2006).

The information that was circulated by the News Feed could be characterized as trivial and was not based on a hierarchy of connectedness; that is, all of the user's friends received the feed regardless of the extent of real-life connectedness. But as boyd (2008) notes, this is the kind of information that has become "the currency of social hierarchy and connectivity" (p. 17). In a way, with the News Feed, what groups were joined or dropped, what romantic relationships were in progress, begun, or ended became virtual gossip. Like all gossip, News Feed is information that is actively spread, but unlike real-world, person-to-person gossip, and because it originates in the user profile, other viewers assume the reliability of this information. boyd contends that regardless of the seemingly inconsequential nature of the information disseminated by the News Feed, users still paid attention to information that had been "previously obscure or difficult to miss (and even harder to forget)" (p. 15), ultimately producing a kind of "cognitive addiction" (p. 17) to trivial social information. Thus it is not surprising to know that undergraduates now enjoy the feed despite their initial misgivings. As privacy features aimed at giving users more control over the feed were implemented, user dissent subsided (Melber, 2008).

Undergraduate users, long aware of data that is hidden by other users, also function in what boyd (2008) calls the "opt-out dynamic" (p. 16). Since News Feed aggregated information without regard for user real-life relationships, now users must consciously decide what they wish to conceal and from whom. Obscuring information about oneself by either hiding it from certain users or just simply not providing that information is a paradoxical phenomenon for college student users. Their generational predisposition is to care about privacy but to be more revealing about self online than previous generations. They appreciate the relative control they have over personal information online yet they are also likely to suspect that the absence of information on others' sites is suspicious. As many of our study's participants noted (recall Matthew), the lack of status information can signal meaning to other users, meaning that is either embedded in online campus social networking norms and relationship status or incredulity.

The social advertising feature, Beacon, which was launched by Facebook in November 2007, released a protest from users similar to that levied as a result of News Feed, this time tapping the older, non-college-user's concerns over the dissemination of private, personal information to businesses and advertisers. Beacon circulated user profile photographs and activities as advertisements for products purchased by Facebook users from a variety of online sites. If a user purchased shoes on Zappos.com or movie tickets from Fandango.com, other users in their friends networks would receive what appeared to be an advertisement for the service. Similarly, sites like NYTimes.com would send Facebook users' stories to other users through the Beacon feature. In a bounded online community in which trust is a governing condition, these purchase announcements were implicit product endorsements without the permission of the buyer/Facebook user. Very quickly, Facebook users began to register complaints about Beacon's violation of their privacy, and within weeks Facebook changed Beacon to be an optional system ("opt-in"), with privacy controls that allow users to turn off or opt out of Beacon completely. Further, Facebook does not store user activity data on those sites.

Users can also opt out of Facebook's collaboration with search engines, Google.com and Yahoo.com. In September 2007, Facebook announced that user profiles in limited view would be indexed by Google and Yahoo unless users modified privacy settings to restrict the dissemination of their data. Facebook profiles indexed on Google and Yahoo and their "public listing" is a link to a limited profile view with a viewable photograph, raising more concerns about user disclosure and privacy. The Google or Yahoo listing contains a thumbnail profile picture and links to interact with the user on Facebook. But again, users must take the initiative to modify their privacy controls to ensure that what is made public by a search engine is in fact information that they have permitted disseminated. To what extent all users—especially all college users—are aware of and use the privacy modifications is not known, though students in our study were certainly conscious of this. Judging by the research on privacy and college student user behavior (Acquisti & Gross, 2006), it's unlikely that the generation for whom privacy is "about controlling how many people know" their personal information (boyd cited in Melber, 2008) will behave differently than they have with other Facebook "social advertising" innovations. For older users, however, their ability to actively control the dissemination of their personal data may well be more important.

Global Growth

According to Computer Industry Almanac, the almost 80% of the world's Internet users reside outside the United States and the above average growth or penetration of the Internet between 2000 and 2008 has occurred in the Middle East, Africa, Asia, and Latin America and the Caribbean. Topping over 1 billion in the first quarter of 2008, Internet use is predicted to increase worldwide yearly from 140 million to 145 million in the next five years, which means that by 2011 or 2012 there will be 2 billion users worldwide. Currently and in the future, much of the growth in Internet use is and will continue to be concentrated in Brazil, Russia, India, and China, countries with large populations. China and India, the only two countries with populations over 1 billion, possess one third of the world's population and show rapid Internet growth usage (Computer Industry Almanac, 2008). As of 2008, China has bested the United States as the number 1 nation in Internet use with 233 million users, a 53% increase from 2007. Though Internet users make up only 17% of China's population compared to the U.S. rate of 71% in 2008, China's rate of growth suggests a continued increase in share of the world's Internet market (MacLeod, 2008). Similar trends are occurring in Latin America and Africa. Despite lower rates of population Internet participation, 22%

and 4.7% respectively, rapid growth in the rates of usage in each region since 2000 affirm their mounting importance in the worldwide Internet market (Computer Industry Almanac, 2008). Wireless access is predicted to account for much of the growth in developing countries in the next five years (Computer Industry Almanac, 2008). In 2008, the average number of languages supported among the world's top 225 websites is 20 (Web Globalization Report Card, 2008).

Online social networking sites are Internet social media with a vast range of tapped and untapped potential for commercial, political, and cultural uses worldwide. With 80% of the world's Internet users outside of the United States, social networking sites like Orkut, hi5, Bebo, MySpace, and Facebook now compete for international audiences. Though established use and growth in membership on these sites varies by region, one trend is clear: the major social networking sites significantly increased their international base in 2007 and continued expansion is assured (ComScore, 2007). According to Datamonitor, social networking sites sustained user growth and will peak in 2009 and plateau by 2012, with much of the significant increase occurring in the Asia Pacific region (2008). By the end of 2007, 89% of membership in Friendster was from the Asia Pacific region, an Internet market in which 43% of its users are social networking site visitors. Bebo attracts 63% of its users from European nations, while Orkut has almost half of its user base in Latin America. The North American user audience is well-established in MySpace and Facebook, with 62% and 68% regional membership respectively (ComScore, 2007). Though each of these regions has experienced positive change in international use in 2007, the most significant change occurred in the Middle East/Africa (+69%), a region in which Internet penetration ranges from 13% to 17% (Computer Industry Almanac, 2008). The social networking site, Tagged.com, has the most internationally balanced audience with 8% of its membership base in each of the international regions (ComScore, 2007). Social networking site preferences are also nation specific. For example, Orkut dominates the Brazilian market; hi5 dominates Peru and Columbia; cyworld dominates South Korea; and LiveJournal dominates Russia (Chang, 2008a).

Operating in 25 different countries, U.S.-based MySpace still captures the largest share of the online social networking market worldwide, logging over 114 million users at the end of 2007. Currently, about 45% of MySpace users are external to the United States, a 72% increase in growth over a one year period (ComScore, 2008). MySpace's reach into countries like Russia, Turkey, Poland, and Portugal reflects the site's ability to support 29 languages, and a conventional site launching strategy that focuses on nationally pertinent information and norms (Chang, 2008b). Setting up offices and staff first in countries targeted for launching, MySpace has rooted its international sites with an eye to cultural and linguistic relevance by making each site ethnically and nationally particular. Beginning in 2006, MySpace began its venture into international markets by establishing its operations in Britain and launching MySpace UK. The MySpace International site offers three regional categorizations—the Americas, Europe, and Asia Pacific. More importantly, however, is that within this regional grouping there is cultural, national, and ethnic specificity. For example, within the Americas, U.S.-identified Latino users can log on to the Spanish language-supported MySpace Latino (U.S.), but a separate and content distinct site for Latinos outside the United States, Latin America (Español) is also available. Spaniards can link to MySpace Spain. For Canadians, a site in English is available, as well as MySpace Canada (Français) that supports Canadian French-language users. In countries like Switzerland with multiple dominant languages, MySpace invites users to log on to Switzerland (Deutsch), Switzerland (Français), and Switzerland (Italiano). A good majority of these MySpace users are now 25 years and older (Jacobs, 2006).

Historically appealing to a niche user community, Facebook's key features have also enabled the site to have wide appeal in two profitable markets: adults over 25 and international users. As an online social network based on existing real-life relationships and community-member trust, Facebook's enhanced privacy controls and bounded community character has enabled its expansion outside of the college and university into other environments. These improved privacy settings can also appeal more directly to particular groups in specific cultural and national settings. For example, women in Pakistan and India, common victims of spamming abuse, are attracted to Facebook's user-control of personal information (Wan, Kumar, &

Bukhari, 2008). But because Facebook's initial and primary language platform has been English, international use has been somewhat constrained. Recognizing the need to increase its global participation, Facebook began its efforts to provide other-than English support for its users when it launched its first non-English site in Spanish in February 2008. Unlike MySpace, however, Facebook did not enter the global, other-than-English market through conventional means. Instead of establishing offices in international markets to embed its production staffers in the culture and language before launching the site, Facebook put out a call to its users to translate the site into Spanish, and to vote on translations before the eventual launch of the site. Users downloaded the Facebook Translation Application to their account and submitted Spanish translations of "poke," "friend," "groups," etc.; then they voted and reached consensus on translations. Though "collaborative translation" is not uncommon in open-source online communities, Facebook's utilization of its own members has drawn criticism from professional translators. Errors in grammar, spelling, and usage were littered throughout the site but despite these problems, Facebook continues to enlist its users to translate the site and has plans for a new language launch every month or so (Hosaka, 2008). By May 2008, users could log onto their accounts in French, German, Italian, Dutch, Polish, Norsk (Norwegian), and Korean. Facebook's international appeal is reflected in its 68 million users outside the United States and its international growth appears to continue. Experiencing much stronger growth in 2000 than MySpace (ComScore, 2008), Facebook has managed to be relevant despite its linguistic gaffes and lack of a culturally embedded launching strategy. As Wan et al. (2008) report, "localization" could well be Facebook's major challenge in the international market, especially within local student culture. Though Facebook has a halo effect for Indian and Pakistani users, as their survey data suggest, the potential for its functions and applications, and even its primary objective, can be at odds with social cultures that directly affect students. Currently, Pakistani and Indian students who study in the United States use Facebook to stay in contact with friends at home, and youth in these countries find it very appealing to join an online social network primarily for U.S. college and university students. But in many other cultures and student groups, membership in social network sites challenges sociocultural and political norms. In Pakistan, for example, Beaconhouse National University in Lahore has blocked Facebook (now the eighth most visited site by Pakistanis) citing it as a distraction to student learning, and in a society in which contact between unmarried young women and young men is prohibited, Facebook is being used by Pakistanis as a virtual "dating" service (Press Trust of India, 2008). Facebook has been blocked in Syria, a predominantly Muslim country prone to censorship after years under military rule. Many suggest that the move to censor Facebook correlates with the recent "cultural awakening" in which concerts, art exhibits, theatrical and movie productions, and academic conferences have been organized (Facthai. wordpress.com, 2007). Al-arabiya.net reported in March 2008 that a prominent Islamic cleric had called for the banning of Facebook because it encouraged women's lustful behavior and was a vehicle of Western immorality. Concerned about the depictions of women's sexuality and homosexuality on Facebook, the cleric demanded the blocking of the website to prevent conflict in Saudi Arabia. In August 2007, a young woman in Riyadh was murdered by her father when he found her communicating with a young man on Facebook (Arab Media & Society, 2008). In Lebanon, four Lebanese university students were jailed for a week for posting remarks on Facebook about a young woman that were perceived vulgar and offensive by her father. The four young men were charged with slander and "violating public morality" (Alarabiya.net, 2008). United Arab Emirates, Mauritius, and Iran have also blocked Facebook (Mashable.com, 2008). Despite government restrictions on Internet access, Cubans living on the Communist-led island have established Facebook accounts. The Cuba network on Facebook boasts over 3,700 members (not all residing in Cuba and many of whom are younger, university educated adults), and topics on the Facebook Discussion include, "que opinan sobre los 50 años de la revolución cubana" (What's your opinion on the 50 years of the Cuban Revolution?").

International political causes have also surfaced on Facebook. In May 2008, spurred on by the success in April 2008 of a Facebook group that called for a nationwide strike to support discontented workers, a Facebook group of activists in Egypt that included university students called for a general strike to protest the government on President Hosni Mubarak's 80th birthday (UKPress.com, 2008). In Bogotá, Colombia, a group of students disenchanted with the leftist guerilla Revolutionary Armed Forces of Colombia (FARC), created a Facebook group and called for marches in 185 cities all over the world to protest FARC kidnappings (Brodzinsky, 2008). The UK-based National AIDS Trust has used Facebook and MySpace since 2006 to disseminate information about World AIDS Day. In 2006, the World AIDS Day was launched on MySpace profile and attracted over 5,000 friends and over 40,000 profiles views. A year later the National AIDS Trust developed a Facebook group to provide information about events in the United Kingdom and the campaign (National AIDS Trust, 2007). On "Facebook Causes," groups exist to raise funds for the Irish Republican Army (IRA), Amnesty International, Greenpeace International, Keep Egypt Clean Project, Fair Trade Certified, WorldVision Malaysia, World AIDS Day, Team Darfur, and Jane Goodall's Roots & Shoots Program among others. Launched as an application specifically intended to "engage" this generation of college and university student users "in seizing the future and making a difference in the world around us," Facebook boldly asserts that this "generation cares deeply, but the current system has alienated" them. To that end, the Facebook Causes application allows the Net Generation to:

> create a cause, recruit their friends into that cause, keep everybody in the cause up-to-speed on issues and media related to the cause, and, most importantly, raise money directly through the cause for any U.S. registered 501(c)(3) nonprofit or Canadian registered charity. [Facebook will] process the donations automatically via credit card, tally the results, and report the donation activity via a public "scorecard" in the cause. (Facebook About Causes, 2008)

Utilizing real-world social networks, Facebook Causes is pitched as a vital part of activism and fundraising, and political demonstration, which has taken on an international character. An application that is the first Facebook Platform Partner of the philanthropic site, Project Agape, Facebook Causes is focused on social justice issues and uses the existing News Feed to alert users in the network about a friend's humanitarian and charitable associations. Online philanthropic giving through social networking sites like Facebook Causes or MySpace Impact is still a small share of the overall share of online donation but like other online charities, it is also expected to increase (Keohane, 2008).

New Niche Users

Graduate students, too, are using Facebook to collaborate on scholarly projects and to exchange professional and personal information. Because Facebook is a bounded online community that provides users with key privacy controls, and because it supports groups within networks, graduate students can use Facebook as a social medium for professional objectives. The demography here, though, is telling. Graduate students (as well as younger faculty) are likely members of generations that are Internet literate and savvy, and some are likely to have had experience with social networking sites as undergraduates and even in high school. As Internet users they are confident and creative, and presuppose that work is collaborative and should not isolate individuals. Graduate student groups have been formed on Facebook representing many disciplines, professions, and sociocultural identities. On groups like the Black Graduate and Professional School Students, the Jordanian Graduate Student Association, the Neuroscience Graduate Student Association at the University of Texas at Austin, and the Association for the Study of Higher Education (ASHE) Graduate Student Network, young preprofessionals communicate and network with other graduate students, share research ideas, exchange and confer about funding opportunities, and trade dissertation stories that sustain and preserve the bounded character of the group. Many graduate students serve as teaching assistants and must negotiate the tricky and somewhat ambiguous territory of Facebook communication with undergraduate students. Many will go on to the professorate, and as the next generation of faculty they will have to think more seriously about their Facebook use as it relates to undergraduate students. That said, one can't help but wonder if the sociocultural norms of online campus social networking culture established in the Net Generation will give these women and men better facility with social nuance online. Perhaps growing up online and having experience with online campus culture and social network sites like Facebook will enable this upcoming faculty generation to better navigate online social norms as professionals.

The presence of college and university faculty on Facebook is a relatively new trend that has raised concerns about professional ethics among the professorate such as: the student–teacher relationship, its uses as an instructional tool, and its relevance to "neomillennial learning styles" (Dede, 2005), as well as its utility as a public relations/recruitment device and information source for academic programs. Unlike graduate students, faculty, regardless of their age and generational characteristics, are compromised in particular ways as online social network users and must exercise care when navigating online campus culture. Though many graduate students are also responsible for undergraduate teaching and advising and thus must consider the power disparity between teachers and students, faculty—because of their unique institutional and professional membership—are obligated to consider more intentionally their use of Facebook in teaching and learning.

Though college and university students in our study as well as in other studies of undergraduates had mixed feelings about faculty presence on Facebook, students generally believe that Facebook is an online social network purposely set up for use by college students (Hewitt & Forte, 2006; Salaway, Katz, Caruso, Kvavik, & Nelson, 2007). College users can feel that their community boundary (student space) has been breeched, and despite privacy controls, that like nonfaculty adult users, faculty are social networking gatecrashers. The province of faculty is perceived as the classroom, the lab, and the academic advice office, and not the online profile. Some students understand the faculty–student relationship as a professional one free of the personal or social (Hewitt & Forte, 2006). The social and personal information that is communicated on Facebook is often characterized by undergraduates as student community-specific, and the site itself as the proverbial student clubhouse to which no faculty are allowed entry. The space is theirs; the rules of communication are theirs. Yet despite the anxiety that some students have about faculty use of Facebook, many students, either because they know how to employ strict privacy controls, or because they feel that they have nothing to hide, are unconcerned about faculty Facebook use. Though women seem less comfortable with faculty presence on Facebook than men do, some students see it as an opportunity to have more access to and communication with faculty (Hewitt & Forte, 2006). The students in our study certainly reflected this view.

From the perspective of the faculty, however, concerns about the nature of the power disparity between student and teacher is of utmost concern. Can what faculty see students doing or communicating bias their perception of the student? What consequence will that have for grading the student's academic performance, advising the student, or writing a letter of reference for the student? What does it mean for a faculty member to "friend" a student or accept a friend request from a student? Do the norms and rules of real-world student–faculty relationships fit the world of online social media and online campus culture? In the prior case, the student may feel undue pressure and intimidation given the power that the faculty has over the student. Unlike the majority of their relationships with friends on their networks, the preexisting, real-life faculty–student relationship is not a peer relationship. The rules and norms of social discourse are different between peers than they are between mentor and apprentice, between advisor and novice learner. Students may feel intimidated or obligated to engage in an online social network relationship with a faculty member simply because they recognize the authority and power resident in the faculty. Much like the conceptualization of harassment in academia and elsewhere, students may feel powerless to refuse the online invitation. Let's recall that most students either do not know the full-range of privacy controls available or just don't activate them, or go along with Facebook's no privacy default setting (Acquisti & Gross, 2006).

The lack of empirical research on the effects of faculty presence on Facebook has not prevented the academic community and the academic professional herself or himself from recognizing that associations with undergraduate students on online social networking sites is ethically ambiguous. University and college faculty have recognized that though they may use Facebook as a means to get to know students in order to strengthen the learning relationship, the personal nature

and generational niche of the online space complicates their intentions. Some faculty like using Facebook to get to know the incoming
first year students assigned to their tutorials or advisory seminars. At
Pepperdine University in California, some faculty use Facebook as
a means of personal communication with students that they believe
helps nurture the faculty–student relationship that is encouraged by
university administration (Reed, 2005). But by all accounts registered
in college and university newspapers, faculty development seminars,
and other media, college faculty using Facebook to communicate with
students do find themselves considering the ethical and pedagogical implications of their online social network use and the impact of
their use on online campus culture. Mark Clague, a member of the
faculty at Michigan State University, has formed a Facebook group
to help faculty negotiate the ethical complications of their use. The
group, "Faculty Ethics on Facebook" presents a "current list" of ethical guidelines that include caveats about using "extreme care with privacy settings," "not spying on students," "never requiring students to
participate," or having their participation "influence a course grade."
Stipulations about "exercising appropriate discretion" when joining
groups (avoid groups with "explicit sexual content or views") and
posting personal communications are featured on the list, as well as a
reminder that faculty should consider the "uneven power dynamics of
the academy" when determining online relationships with students.
Pedagogically, faculty is advised to maintain "official course activities"
off of Facebook, and "never posting official course communication"—
assignment grades, comments, reactions—on the site. Like all other
Facebook groups "Faculty Ethics on Facebook" is intended to be an
ongoing, discussion generating collaboration. Thus, in the coming
years, we will see the evolutionary changes of the deliberation. We
will likely see whether and to what extent the norms, conventions, and
regulations that shape and govern real-world faculty–student interactions are adopted, reshaped, or abandoned on online social networking spaces. We will see to what extent, if any, faculty use changes
online campus culture.

In many ways these concerns are borne of the cultural shift brought
on by technology and online social media. In previous generations,
faculty and students communicated primarily in class and outside of

class conversations were conducted in faculty offices or in public campus spaces typically within the confines of a sanctioned curricular or extracurricular activity. Since the 1990s, however, faculty and student communication has expanded to include electronic mail and online course management tools like Blackboard, WebCT, Virtual-U, and Learning Space. Each of these computer mediated communication technologies has made it necessary for academic faculty to modify or simply transfer traditional modes and norms of real-life academic and pedagogical communication online. Additionally, these technologies have revived debates about the historic division between the academic or curricular aspects of campus life, and the social or extracurricular spaces of college students.

The extent to which faculty transition to computer-mediated communication with students or how faculty behaves as virtual communicators affecting online campus culture is little studied, but research has suggested that the use of e-mail by faculty, for example, is related to individual faculty differences. Faculty with positive attitudes toward innovation and change, and who have technological self-efficacy, are very likely to use e-mail (Minsky & Marin, 1999), and data from the 2004 National Study of Postsecondary Faculty suggest that at least 30% of all faculty in all fields use e-mail and the Internet (Meyer & Xu, 2007). These same data also suggest that some disciplinary differences occur in faculty use of technology, with faculty in the humanities and the natural sciences having higher rates of use than all other faculty, and that perhaps the recent emphasis on technology in doctoral education is responsible for higher-use rates among faculty (Meyer & Xu, 2007). Though age did not appear to be a factor in the survey of faculty in 2004, others have found that age was an important predictor of faculty self-efficacy and interest in using digital technologies (Benson & Mekolichick, 2007; Xu & Meyer, 2007). The strong relationship between faculty's conceptions of self, their motivation to use technology, and their effectiveness as instructional users is positively correlated with faculty interest and effectiveness, suggesting that technology use is intertwined with faculty's professional identity (Benson & Mekolichick, 2007). As sociologists Benson and Mekolichick (2007) note, faculty appear to have "integrated the use of digital technology into their sense of self" and that at some level the ability of faculty to use technology has become part of their own pedagogical expectations of their faculty role (p. 506). Even faculty productivity measures (publication, service, and teaching) are positively correlated with technology use suggesting that either the use of technology like email and the Internet improve faculty productivity or that normally productive faculty use these technologies to improve their scholarly production and pedagogical commitments (Xu & Meyer, 2007).

Online campus culture is also informed by students' use of online course management systems that organize their courses. Though not social online media, online course technologies add another dimension to students' online habits and customs, and explicitly inject faculty into online interactions with students. Online course management systems like Blackboard, WebCT, Virtual-U, and Learning Space are now ubiquitous on college and university campuses and the expectation that faculty use this technology in their teaching is now the norm. Several years ago EDUCAUSE Center for Applied Research sponsored an empirical study of the use of course management systems by faculty in the University of Wisconsin system to determine the extent of faculty use, the factors that motivate faculty use, the purposes for which these systems are used by faculty, and what gains in learning could be associated with their use. The data reveal that faculty is motivated to use this technology less as a means for improving pedagogy or student learning and more as a tool of organizing and managing teaching duties and responsibilities. Reflecting their general generational perspective on the purpose of technology (to make real-world work more efficient), faculty adopts this technology to give students access to course documents like syllabi and required readings, to expedite the delivery of grades to students, and to easily communicate with students. Faculty will supplement class materials, include more interactive tools (discussion groups, wikis, etc.), and communicate more with students through this technology, though this is not to say that these communications are social in nature. Faculty–student communication through online course management systems are circumscribed by their academic and not social intentions. Faculty has also been provoked to use online course management systems through administrative incentives (faculty development/training; merit based pay and performance review) but not by their perception of student demands or needs for academic technology. However, as faculty used online course management interfaces more and more, they began to identify more uses for their teaching. Over time, use in one class increased faculty perception of how such technology could be used in another class. It is almost as if once embedded in the culture of technology, faculty are better able to appreciate its wider range of uses, or more to the point, are better able to switch generation use paradigms. As faculty become more culturally literate in the uses of technology, the more they begin to conceptualize in the culture of technology. A very small minority of faculty in this study (5%) felt that these online systems were difficult to use and were too time-consuming (Morgan, 2003). It appears, then, that faculty whether self-motivated or prompted by professional expectations, may be poised to accept the reach of new technologies, perhaps even social media.

In an effort to bridge academic activities on course management technology with students' social networking behavior, the course management platform, Blackboard, has developed a Facebook application that taps into students' social networking habits. Blackboard Sync (released May 2008) will distribute course information and updates to students' Facebook accounts (Guess, 2008). A Facebook application, Blackboard Sync will send to students weekly class announcements, post new content items and notification of new grades, and will contain a course roster and syllabus. The aim, according to Blackboard, is to create learning networks or classmate networks that foster "social learning opportunities" (BlackboardSync.com). The application is intended to connect classmates with each other so that they can engage in both online and offline collaborations and study groups. Privacy will still prevail in this application. Only students enrolled in a specific course will be able to view course announcements and postings, and access to grades will be user specific. Obviously, the educational goal of this interface between academic and a social networking technologies is to get the curriculum into the extracurriculum; the academic into students' social spaces wherever they may be. Given the ubiquity of social networking in campus culture, disseminating academic information to students more broadly, more efficiently and more effectively seems reasonable. The desire to craft learning opportunities outside the classroom is not new in higher education but what is evident in this particular venture is the direct intrusion of academic expectations and demands in student social space. To what extent students will feel that this violates the spirit of social networking has yet to be decided. Clearly, because students can now access and utilize technology with relatively few restrictions, it seems reasonable to expect that all that happens on a college campus will likely be integrated on social networking platforms. Students like Teresa in our study already use Facebook for such things as searching for classmates and networking about class assignments.

Since the 1980s and 1990s, colleges and universities in the United States almost doubled their levels of information technology expenditures (Green, 2004). The EDUCAUSE 2007 Core Data Survey explains this increase in its finding that faculty support in the use of technology in teaching and learning has increased significantly across all dimensions since the previous year (p. 32). These same survey data indicate that 71% of faculty across all institution types surveyed use online course management systems "selectively" (p. 36). But though a university's information technology expenditures is not solely dedicated to academic or instructional computing, the trend is to give more focus to the formal use of technologies in undergraduate and graduate education, a trend that will require institutions and the academic profession to reframe or reconstitute the traditional linear faculty–student teacher–learner relationship. Instead of simply using online technologies to aid in the management of courses, faculty will likely transition to combining time-honored instruction with new forms of online instruction like wireless learning and social networking sites (Chronicle of Higher Education, 2008; Dieterle & Dede, 2007; Morgan, 2003). These new forms of instruction that are conducted in and through information technologies such as social networking sites will mean that the faculty's professional identity will experience challenges to its instructional autonomy and knowledge-making authority. With its emphasis on active, multiple source learning, these technologies challenge the historic instructional autonomy and authority of the professor. Online social media's collaborative and democratic nature has the potential to redistribute the power of expertise so that the faculty–student teaching–learning relationship is not so strictly linear. Social networking technologies can transform courses to a student-centered model, averting some of the disadvantages of the teacher-centered model traditionally found in higher education. In this direction, "ubiquitous computing"—technology that is always accessible and is not restricted to a particular place—has significant advantages, especially for the Internet and Web 2.0 generations of college students (Kolomvatsos, 2007). Portable, accessible, and efficient, social networking technologies have the potential to enhance college student learning. For the "neo-millennial learner," the growth and expansion of instructional information technologies like online social networks will correspond to their communal approach to learning (Dede, 2005). These advances in academic technology will enable the Internet student generations to "balance experiential learning, guided mentoring and collective reflection," and communicate through "nonlinear, associational webs of representations" (p. 7) no doubt affecting an online campus culture.

As is already evident and logically evolutionary, younger scholars and graduate students preparing to enter the academic profession have already started to make this transition. Perhaps these generations of scholars and teachers will not need to make paradigmatic shifts in their professional identities as instructors and knowledge authorities, but they will have to contend with the complicated and thorny relationship between instructional technologies and commercial and managerial aims. As noted by Selwyn (2007) and Stahl (2004), faculty must be aware of the commercial interests in the adoption of e-teaching technologies and to what extent these aims compromise the integrity of the student–faculty face-to-face instructional relationship. The adoption of course management systems effectively restricts the instructor to the commercial entity's conception and engineering of pedagogy. The pedagogical tools course management systems that are offered to faculty to all intents and purposes are an implicit restriction of the faculty's autonomy over instructional decision making. Further, if a central claim of these technologies is to improve the efficiency and frequency of faculty–student communication, it stands to reason that faculty should wonder about the effects on the quality of the interactions. Despite Xu and Meyer's (2007) finding that faculty productivity was positively correlated with faculty information technology use, and the de facto corporatization of the university and the reshaping of the faculty as entrepreneurs (Slaughter & Leslie, 1997), all faculty must consider how institutional administrators and managers will levy the use of instructional technology as a measure of faculty productivity and performance devoid of pedagogical regard. Could these systems serve as yet another means to make faculty more accountable for their teaching?

In other sectors of the university like alumni relations and development, online social networking sites, especially Facebook, have already impacted operations. The deep penetration of sites like Facebook and LinkedIn in the more recent college and university alumni classes have presented alumni relations offices with opportunities to expand their alumni base and improve their data gathering. Class reunions, like on-campus parties, can be organized on Facebook. Whether choosing to develop institution-specific sites or using Facebook to complement institutional virtual alumni sites, alumni associations now consider online social networking in their fund raising and professional networking activities. In one of New York State's public universities, the Binghamton University Alumni Association, for example, dedicates much of its online efforts to B-Connected, its online alumni community, but supplements its alumni information collection through its Facebook Group of over 900 members and a growing list of specific affinity alumni groups (members of the college newspaper, *Binghamton Alumni in Boston*, etc.; Binghamton Alumni Association, 2007). Individual alumni use these sites to reconnect with classmates and the college or university, and some alumni use these sites for professional or career development. Alumni seeking employment can now use Facebook to identify fellow alums currently working at particular companies and in turn, companies can tap into alumni groups on Facebook to recruit potential employees. Many university alumni association officers (like Harvard's, for example), use Facebook in precisely this way.

As we noted in the previous chapter, online social networking sites like Facebook have now also proven to be effective tools in campus emergencies. In a recent study of the use of social media during the Virginia Tech University shooting April 2007, traditional mass media were found unreliable. Internet users in each case were better able to communicate critical information faster than conventional media. Instant messaging on Twitter and a Facebook user group called I'm OK at VT displayed the latest information (Palen, 2008). This is not surprising given the mobile and wireless capabilities of users, as well as the daily regularity of online social networking use. College and university students are frequent users and have an established and robust pattern of use. Researchers have found that digital communication typically happens while students are engaged in school work. College student use of computer-mediated communication on Facebook increases during study hours and generally correlates with their daily routines (Golder, Wilkinson, & Huberman, 2006). Thus, while on campus students will most likely receive or send emergency messages through online means, whether Facebook or other social networking sites. With the development of global positioning satellite capabilities on mobile devices, college students will be especially capable of sending and receiving the latest information on emergency and disaster conditions to authorities, administrators, and parents.

New applications and functions appear on social networking sites very regularly and reflect the growing online user needs, as well as the subtle intrusion of commercial entities. Since May 2007, Facebook has opened its platform to external applications developers and has since expanded their applications exponentially. Now numbering over 24,000 with 140 added per day, the norm for Facebook is the third-party developed application (*Facebook Statistics*, 2008). Externally developed applications dominate the site with top user preferences in business, chatting, dating, "Just for Fun," messaging, sports and utility categories. New in 2008 is the real-time application, "Chat!" that allows members to chat online in various rooms. Like all Facebook applications, "Chat!" is chronicled in the News Feed and Mini-Feed applications on user profiles. An Online Friends icon appears in the lower right-hand corner of the Facebook profile page toolbar to indicate how many and who among the user's friends is currently online and available for chatting. In April 2008, Facebook added the new "life-casting" feature that automatically updates the mininews feed. "Life-casting" is the new means to continuously transmit personal action and events on social media. New sites like Twitter.com are dedicated to life-casting or "sousveillance"—the real-life experience from the individual's point of view described and sometimes captured in digital images or video and broadcast as microblogging. External application development for Facebook had slowed in the first months of 2008 perhaps as a reflection of the increased competition from Google's OpenSocial interface launched in November 2007. A common interface for social networking applications, any application developed on OpenSocial will be able to operate on any online social networking site that supports it. To date, MySpace, hi5, Bebo, Friendster, and Orkut all support OpenSpace developed applications. Though Facebook has announced that it will not join OpenSpace (Helft, 2008), it has responded with Facebook Connects, portability technology that will enable Facebook members to transfer and connect their profile data to other Internet sites. Conscious of its primary niche concern and market need—user privacy control—Facebook will develop technology that will allow for authentic member data portability, assuring users of the privacy controls and security. Photos, friends, and events posted on Facebook profiles can be transmitted to other sites, effectively reducing user time spent constructing new profiles and entering data on those sites. How these new developments and applications will change or shape online campus culture is yet to be determined. But as we have seen from our students' testimonies, students' online campus culture is not static. Rather, the online campus culture described by the participants in our study is organic and complex, and evolves with each new application and technological advancement.

Do these new technologies and applications meet Facebook's bounded community user needs? Has Facebook's "walled-garden" approach to social networking been weakened and challenged by these new technologies and business partnerships? When Facebook announced its exclusive third-party advertising platform partnership with Microsoft October 2007, executives described the affiliation as "a strong statement of our confidence in the long-term economics of this partnership" (Facebook Press Release, 2007). Motivated by the growing international markets and escalating capabilities by other social networking sites, Facebook crafted an advertising strategy with Microsoft that effectively converted their niche users into online social graph product promoters. Now embedded in users' social graph activities—their posts, News Feeds, etc.—product promotion typically promoted in real-life by word of mouth between friends and family, was now disseminated digitally across user networks. Though Facebook pulled back from its initial structuring of its primary advertising application, Beacon, by allowing users to opt out, users have become increasingly aware that Facebook is no longer the tight, bounded, online niche community it once was. Through the partnership, businesses can create profiles open to user interaction. Within a month of the announced partnership, over 100,000 business profiles had been launched on Facebook (Catone, 2007). Users can access business profiles like "Cribfinder," a real estate group sponsored by Jenius Industries. Facebook users can check out Facebook network users' restaurant reviews on either "LocalPicks" sponsored by TripAdvisor.com or "Zagat Ratings and Reviews" sponsored by the celebrated Zagat Survey. Users looking for employment or professional advancement opportunities can log on to groups sponsored by CareerBuilder.com on Facebook, "Find a Better Job" or "Canadian Jobs." Together with the social advertisements disseminated through the user-controlled Beacon feature, Facebook as a vehicle for target advertising is in fact firmly established.

College and university student response to the intrusion of commercial advertising is mixed, some surrendering to its inevitability, while others opt out as best they can. Students are also conscious, though perhaps to varying degrees, that Facebook's advertising strategy is simply the digital manifestation of their actual real-world communication, ironically one of the site's most appealing features to the demographic. The students in this study tell us that any distaste for advertising is still not enough to get them to leave Facebook. It is too much a part of campus culture—the pull is just too strong. In point of fact, students "sell" each other lots of things through their real-life exchanges—the movies they enjoy, the music they download, the clothing that they wear. Branding is a long-established practice internationally. Wearing Adidas sneakers and Abercrombie & Fitch sweatshirts, using iPods are all marketing behaviors in the real world. And though college students are generally unaware (or don't care about) product country of origin (Anderson Analytics, 2007), they have effectively become unpaid marketers of goods and services. The Apple logo displayed on a student's iPod or Starbuck's Greek mythological sea siren logo that now seductively calls students to drink lattes and mochachinos, epitomize the free, real-world attitude branding and marketing that is now embedded in the digital, virtual social graph. To what extent college and university students and other new adult users will resist and defend against the commercialization of online social networking space is still undecided. Despite assurances to maintain user privacy and user autonomy, Facebook seems poised to continue transport the real-world in all of its manifestation to the social world online—the most salient building block of online social media in the early part of this century.

Postscript

We are indebted to the many, many undergraduate students who thoughtfully communicated with us their excitement for and anxieties about the hybrid space of online college culture and friendship. These students welcomed us into their "walled garden" of online social networking and revealed the unmistakable promise of social media for current and future generations of college students. Like college student generations before them, this generation of expert online social networking users are confident and mindful of the power of connections that link their real and virtual lives. Our students easily progressed onto each new online social network capability, each new wrinkle in their ability to control personal information and access friends' communications. Our students readily improved their online fluency and with time developed their awareness of the role that these virtual spaces played in their real-world living. We noted that their activity and consumption of online social media proved much more productive than problematic, and believe that their continued use will follow a similar developmental course. Though the current zeitgeist of college and university students, it's not unimaginable or irrational to believe that the culture of online sociability will continue to extend beyond the college years into students' future adult worlds of business, family, community and commerce. Unlike some historic collegiate fads and trends, online social networking broadly conceived will endure. We anticipate that colleges and universities will work toward more formal integration of social networking sites like Facebook into campus academic and social activities and its particular campus identity. On some campuses, this is already the case. Much as campuses incorporated student activities and groups as part of the intellectual and cultural climate of the institution, so too will they unite student spaces real and virtual. That is, in our view, the future of campus culture.

Glossary

AIM (AOL Instant Messenger): Real-time instant messaging; Facebook users can submit their AIM usernames and password and match AIM buddies to Facebook members.

Albums: Photographs can be shared on Facebook's Photos application by grouping them into albums. Users can enter data that name an album, give the location of the photos, and a description. Albums can be restricted to particular users. Photos in albums can be tagged or untagged. See TAG.

Applications: Computer software that directly utilizes the capacities of the computer to perform a task. These are programs within Facebook (developed either by Facebook or other third-party software developers) that are easy to install and allow users to complete a number of tasks from posting photos to planning events to playing games such as an online version of scrabble.

Closed profile: Member profiles that are accessible only to those given permission by the user.

Events: An application that allows Facebook users to search, browse, create, and RSVP to real-world events.

> *Closed events:* All Facebook members can see a description of the posted event but adding a name to the guest list requires an invitation. Users can request an invitation from the event administrator (the user who created the event) who is the only user who can create the guest list.

> *Open events:* Accessible by all Facebook members; users can add their own name to the guest list.

> *Secret events:* Invitations are received by Facebook notification or e-mail only to specific Facebook members.

Facebook:
1. (noun): The online social networking site.
2. (verb): To engage and participate in the online social networking site.

Facebook status:

1. *Relationship status*: Within the Profile Relationships settings, users can choose to indicate whether they are "Single," "In a Relationship," "Engaged," "Married," "It's Complicated," or "In an Open Relationship."
2. *Status*: A short, open-ended statement that users post for their friends to see.

Friend:

1. (noun): To be a part of a user's social network or Friends List.
2. (verb): To extend the invitation to be a part of a user's social network; to accept the invitation to be on a Friends List.

Friend request: An invitation to be added to a user's Friends List that is sent to the member's e-mail and that appears on the profile page under "Requests." Users can ignore requests or confirm the request.

Group: A Facebook application that allows a collection of Facebook users to form an affinity network of users to information.

Impression management: The idea that certain information is a signal or indicator of something that identifies the online user; a term coined by boyd and Ellison (2007).

Limited profile: A means of controlling the Facebook profile information viewed, users can create a bare-bones profile to show to particular users.

Message: A private text communication that can be sent to any Facebook member even if not on a user's Friend List or on the user's networks.

Mini-feed: A chronicle of the Facebook user's activities that appears on the user's profile page and is seen only by those who can see the user's profile page.

Network: The set of connections or associations defined by college or university, high school or workplace, or geographic location that constitutes a member group and is designated by an e-mail address. Network users can give each other permission to see their profile information even it they are not friends.

News feed: Automatic updates of friends' activities that appear on the profile page and user inbox. Users can customize but not opt-out of the feed.

Open profile: Member profiles that allow access to any Facebook member.

Poke: An online Facebook prod or nudge of another user to signal a desire to communicate.

Post: To send or place a text or image communication on Facebook.

Privacy: Facebook settings that allow users to determine what information is visible to which user.

Profile: The Facebook member's webpage; a basic profile is created automatically based on the information entered when registering.

Profile picture: The photograph of the user that appears on her or his main Facebook page. A question mark is displayed by Facebook if a user does not upload a photograph on the main profile page.

Stalking: Browsing or searching for other users and their posted activities on Facebook. Not to be confused with the non-Internet use of the term to mean obsessive pursuit, harassment.

Tag: A way of associating a person with a photograph posted on Facebook. The names of the persons in the photograph appear over the online image. To get rid of the association or the "tag," users can "untag" or "detag" themselves so that names no longer appear on the images.

Unfriend (verb): To remove a user from the Friends List.

Wall: A place on the Facebook profile page where friends can write messages, send applications, and communicate information. Only friends can write on each other's walls.

References

Acquisti, A., & Gross, R. (2006). *Imagined communities: Awareness, information sharing, and privacy on the Facebook. Pre-proceedings version.* Paper
presented at Privacy Enhancing Technologies Workshop (PET).

Alarabiya.net (2008). Facebook insults send 4 Lebanese boys to jail.
Retrieved March 30, 2008 from http://www.alarabiya.net/save_print.
php?print=1&cont_id=44325&lang=en

Alexa.com (2008). Global top 500. Retrieved January 30, 2008, from http://
www.alexa.com/site/ds/top_sites?ts_mode=global&lang=none

American Council on Education. (1994). The student personnel point of view.
In A. L. Rentz (Ed.), *Student affairs: A profession's heritage.* Lanham,
MD: American College Personnel Association.

Anderson Analytics. (2007). It's from where? College students clueless on
where favorite brands come from. Retrieved November 27, 2007, from
http://www.andersonanalytics.com/newsfiles/20070524.htm

Anderson, B. (1998). *Imagined communities: Reflection on the origin and spread
of nationalism* (Rev. ed.). London: Verso.

Anderson, K. (2001). Internet use among college students: An exploratory
study. *Journal of American College Health, 50*(1), 21–26.

Anderson, S., & Rainie, L. (2006). The future of the internet II. PEW Internet and American Life Project. Retrieved September 26, 2007, from
http://www.pewinternet.org/PPF/r/188/report_display.asp

Arab Media and Society. (2008). Preacher demands blocking of Facebook
due to Saudi women access. Retrieved May 13, 2008, from http://www.
arabmediasociety.com/arab_media_wire/?item=654

Arnett, J. (2000, May). Emerging adulthood: A theory of development from
the late teens through the twenties. *American Psychologist, 55,* 469–480.

Arrington, M. (2005). 85% of college students use Facebook. Retrieved
August 16, 2007, from http://www.techcrunch.com/2005/09/07/85-of-
college-students-use-facebook/

Attinasi, L. C. (1989). Getting in: Mexican Americans' perceptions of university attendance and the implications for freshman year persistence.
The Journal of Higher Education, 60(3), 247–277.

Auchard, E. (2007). It's no secret: Facebook's allure is its privacy.
Retrieved September 26, 2007, from http://www.reuters.com/article/
technologyNews/idUSN1529632920070715

Bailenson, J. N., Yee, N., Blascovich, J., & Guadagno, R. E. (in press). Trans-
formed social interaction in mediated interpersonal communication. In
E. Konijn, M. Tanis, , S. Utz, & A. Linden (Eds.), *Mediated interpersonal communication* (pp. 106–123). New York: Erlbaum.

Barnes, S. B. (2006, September). A privacy paradox: Social networking in the United States. First Monday, 11(9). Retrieved September 9, 2007 from http://www.firstmonday.org/issues/issue11_9/barnes/index.html

Baudrillard, J. (1983). *Simulations*. Cambridge, MA: MIT Press.

Baudrillard, J. (2001). Symbolic exchange and death. In *Jean Baudrillard: Selected writings* (M. Poster, Ed.). Stanford, CA: Stanford University Press.

Baym, N. K. (1998). The emergence of on-line community. In S. G. Jones (Ed.), *Cybersociety 2.0: Revisiting computer-mediated communication and community* (pp. 35–68). Thousand Oaks, CA: Sage.

Benson, D. E., & Mekolichick, J. (2007). Conceptions of self and the use of digital technologies in a learning environment. *Education, 127*(4), 498–510.

Binghamton Alumni Association. (2007). Check out the Binghamton alumni group on Facebook. Retrieved July 9, 2007, from http://alumni.bighamton.edu/AC/june07/TopStories/Facebook.htm

Blackboard Sync. (2008). Retrieved May 15, 2008, from http://wiki.blackboardsync.com/display/SYNC/Home

boyd, d. m. (2004, April 24–29). *Friendster and publicly articulated social networks*. Paper presented at Conference on Human Factors and Computing Systems (CHI 2004), Vienna.

boyd, d. m. (2007). Why youth (heart) social network sites: The role of networked publics in teenage social life. In D. Buckingham (Ed.), *MacArthur Foundation Series on Digital Learning: Youth, identity, and digital media* (pp. 119–142). Cambridge, MA: MIT Press.

boyd, d. m. (2008). Facebook's privacy train wreck: Exposure, invasion, and social convergence. Convergence: The *International Journal of Research into New Media Technologies, 14*(1), 13–20.

boyd, d. m., & Ellison, N. (2007). Social network sites: Definition, history, and scholarship. *Journal of Computer-Mediated Communication, 13*(1), article 11.

Brodzynski, S. (2008). Internet site to spawn protests in 185 cities Monday against rebel group's methods. Retrieved February 4, 2008, from http://www.csmonitor.com/2008/0204/p04s02-woam.html

Bugeja, M. J. (2006). Facing the Facebook. *The Chronicle of Higher Education*. Retrieved August 26, 2007, from http://chronicle.com/jobs/2006/01/2006012301c.htm

Butler, J. (1990). *Gender trouble: Feminism and the subversion of identity. Thinking Gender*. New York: Routledge.

Byrne, D. (2008). The future of (the) "race": Identity, discourse and the rise of computer-mediated public spheres. In A. Everett (Ed.), MacArthur Foundation Series on Digital Learning: Vol. *Race and ethnicity* (pp. 15–38). Cambridge, MA: MIT Press.

Catone, J. (2007). Facebook unveils ad strategy—Users become marketers. Retrieved November 6, 2007, from http://www.readwriteweb.com/archives/facebook_unveils_ad_strategy.php

Chang, M. (2008a). Social networks and international audiences. Retrieved April 18, 2008, from http://www.16thletter.com/2008/04/16/social-networks-and-international-audiences/

Chang, M. (2008b). Facebook vs. MySpace: The battle for global social network dominance. Retrieved April 18, 2008, from http://www.the-standard.com/news/2008/04/16/facebook-vs-myspace-battle-global-social-network-dominance

Chronicle of Higher Education. (2008). IT on campus: What the future holds. Retrieved on April 4, 2008, from http://chronicle.com/weekly/v54/i30/30b00601.htm#trends

Classmates.com (2008). Retrieved May 18, 2008, from http://www.class-mates.com/

Cohen, E. (2007a). Young women drink, party, post. Retrieved December 11, 2007, from http://cnn.site.printthis.clickability.com

Cohen, N. (2007b). Brawl over Islam on Facebook. *The New York Times*. Retrieved September 10, 2007, from http://www.nytimes.com/2007/09/10/technology/10facebook.html?sq=facebook%20september%2010%20 2007%20&st=nyt&adxnnl=1&scp=4&adxnnlx=1210597348-sLaeQ+E+1e4phu0R7+AhUw

Computer Industry Almanac. (2008). Retrieved April 5, 2008, from http://www.internetworldstats.com/stats.htm.

ComScore. (2007). Social networking goes global: Major social networking sites substantially expanded their global visitor base during past year. Retrieved July 31, 2007, from http://www.comscore.com/press/release.asp?press=1555

ComScore. (2008). Measuring the digital world. Retrieved May 15, 2008, from http://www.comscore.com

Creswell, J. W. (2007). *Qualitative inquiry and research design: Choosing among five approaches* (2nd ed.). Thousand Oaks, CA: Sage.

Datamonitor. (2008). The future of social networks. Retrieved February 24, 2008, from http://www.datamonitor.com/industries/research/?pid=D MTC2155&type=Report

Dede, C. (2005). Planning for neomillennial learning styles. EDUCAUSE. Retrieved August 26, 2007, from http://connect.educause.edu/Library/EDUCAUSE+Quarterly/PlanningforNeomillennialL/39899

De Vise, D. (2008). Schoolyard face-offs blamed on Facebook taunts. *The Washington Post Online*. Retrieved April 27, 2008, from www.washing-tonpost.com/wp-dyn/content/article/2008/04/26/AR2008042601286.html

DeVoss, D. N., & Selfe, C. L. (2002). "This page under construction": Reading women shaping online identities. *Pedagogy: Critical Approaches to Teaching literature, Language, Composition and Culture, 2*(1), 31–48.

Dieterle, E., & Dede, C. (2007). "Neomillennial" learning styles propagated by wireless handheld devices. In M. D. Lytras & Naeve, A. (Eds.). *Ubiquitous and pervasive knowledge and learning management: Semantics, social networking and new media to their full potential* (pp. 35–66). Hershey, PA: Idea Group.

Donath, J. S. (1999). Identity and deception in the virtual community. In P. Kollock & M. Smith (Eds.), *Communities in cyberspace* (pp. 22–29). New York: Routledge.

Donath, J. S., & boyd, d. m. (2004). Public displays of connection. *BT Technology Journal, 22*(4), 70–82.

EDUCAUSE. (2007). EDUCAUSE core data survey. Retrieved January 2, 2007, from http://www.educause.edu/ir/library/pdf/pub8004e.pdf

Ellison, N. B., Steinfield, C., & Lampe, C. (2007). The benefits of Facebook "friends:" Social capital and college students' use of online social network sites. *Journal of Computer-Mediated Communication, 12*(4), article 1. Retrieved December 8, 2007, from http://jcmc.indiana.edu/vol12/issue4/ellison.html

Emirbayer, M., & Goodwin, J. (1994). Network analysis, culture, and the problem of agency. *The American Journal of Sociology, 99*(6), 1411–1454.

Evans, N. J., Forney, D. S., & Guido-DiBrito, F. (1998). *Student development in college: Theory, research, and practice.* San Francisco: Jossey-Bass.

Facebook about Causes. (2008). Retrieved April 30, 2008, from http://apps.facebook.com/causes/about

Facebook Press Release. (2007). Facebook and Microsoft expand strategic alliance. Retrieved October 25, 2007, from http://www.facebook.com/press/releases.php?p=8084

Facebook Press Release. (2008a). Facebook releases site in Spanish; German and French to follow. Retrieved February 7, 2008, from http://www.facebook.com/press/releases.php?p=16446

Facebook Press Release. (2008b). Facebook updates privacy controls. Retrieved March 18, 2008, from http://www.facebook.com/press/releases.php?p=24114

Facebook Statistics. (2008). Retrieved May 8, 2008, from http://www.facebook.com/press/info.php?statistics

Facebook use continues to skyrocket. (n.d.). Retrieved July 9, 2007, from http://www.insidefacebook.com/2007/07/06/facebook-use-continues-to-skyrocket/

Facthai.wordpress.com (2007). Syria: A slap in the Face(book)-global voice. Retrieved December 8, 2007, from http://facthai.wordpress.com/2007/11/20/syria-a-slap-in-the-facebook-global-voice/

Flowers, L., Pascarella, E. T., & Pierson, C. T. (2000). Information technology use and cognitive outcomes in the first year of college. *Journal of Higher Education, 71*(6), 637–667.

Fox, S., & Livingston, G. (2007). Latinos online. PEW Internet and American Life Project. Retrieved April 7, 2007, from http://www.pewinternet.org/pdfs/Latinos_Online_March_14_2007.pdf

Freeman, L. C. (2004). *The development of social network analysis: A study in the sociology of science.* Vancouver: Empirical Press.

Fuller, A. (2006). Employers snoop on Facebook. Retrieved November 27, 2007, from http://daily.stanford.edu/article/2006/1/20/employersSnoopOnFacebook

Gergen, K. (1991). *The saturated self: Dilemmas of identity in contemporary life.* New York: Basic Books.

Golder, S., Wilkinson, D., & Huberman, B. (2006). Rhythms of social interaction: Messaging within a massive online network. Retrieved March 4, 2008, from http://www.hpl.hp.com/research/idl/papers/facebook/facebook.pdf

Green, K. C. (2004). Trust, but verify. Retrieved September 30, 2004, from http://campustechnology.com/printarticle.aspx?id=39975

Grossman, L. (2007). Why Facebook is the future. *Time Magazine.* Retrieved August 26, 2007, from http://www.time.com/time/magazine/article/0,9171,1655722,00.html

Guess, A. (2008). Facebook, meet Blackboard. Retrieved May 14, 2008, from http://www.insidehighered.com/news/2008/05/14/sync

Hargittai, E. (2007). Whose space? Differences among users and non-users of social network sites. *Journal of Computer-Mediated Communication, 13*(1), article 14. Retrieved January 2, 2008, from http://jcmc.indiana.edu/vol13/issue1/hargittai.html

Hass, N. (2006). You're your Facebook.com. *The New York Times.* Retrieved October 16, 2007, from http://www.nytimes.com/2006/01/08/education/edlife/facebooks.html?scp=1&sq=facebook+campus+police&st=nyt.

Helft, M. (2008). Yahoo is joining an alliance on social networks. *The New York Times.* Retrieved March 26, 2008, from http://www.nytimes.com/2008/03/26/technology/26open.html?sq=opensocial&st=nyt&adxnnl=1&scp=2&adxnnlx=1210415224-Q4tNNW1plYLwzw+lt3O0Hg

Hersh, S. A., & Hinkle, S. E. (2007). Shaping the Facebook of higher education: Teaching online street smarts during new student orientation. Presented at the ACPA/NASPA Joint Meeting, Orlando, FL.

Hewitt, A., & Forte, A. (2006, November 4–8). *Crossing boundaries: Identity management and Student/faculty relationships on the Facebook.* Paper presented at CSCW 2006, Banff, Alberta, Canada.

Horrigan, J. (2008). Mobile access to data and information. PEW Internet and American Life Project. Retrieved April 12, 2008, from http://www.pewinternet.org/pdfs/PIP_Mobile.Data.Access.pdf

Hosaka, T. A. (2008). Lost in translation? Facebook getting free labor but some say its global project spells trouble. Retrieved April 30, 2008, from http://ap.google.com/article/ALeqM5hfp5JdnNee3FfmKog-USTeqDb2nwD904DTHO0

InsideFacebook.com (2007). Facebook use continue to skyrocket. Retrieved July 6, 2007, from http://www.insidefacebook.com/2007/07/06/facebook-use-continues-to-skyrocket/

Jacobs, D. (2006). Different online social networks draw different age groups: Report. Retrieved October 6, 2007, from http://www.ibtimes.com/articles/20061007/myspace-friendster-xanga-facebook.htm

Jones, S. G. (Ed.). (1995). *Cybersociety: Computer-mediated communication and community.* Thousand Oaks, CA: Sage.

Jones, S. G. (Ed.). (1998). *Cybersociety 2.0: Revisiting computer-mediated communication and community.* Thousand Oaks, CA: Sage.

Jones, S. G. (2002). The internet goes to college: How students are living in the future with today's technology. Pew Internet & American Life Project. Retrieved August 16, 2007, from http://www.pewinternet.org/

Jordan, T. (1999). Cyberpower: The culture and the politics of cyberspace and the internet. London: Routledge.

Katz, J. E., & Rice, R. E. (2002). *Social consequences of internet use: Access, involvement, and interaction.* Cambridge, MA: MIT Press.

Keohane, G. L. (2008). The Facebook philanthropos: How much giving do online contests really generate? Retrieved February 12, 2008, from http://www.slate.com/id/2183542/

Knowledge@Wharton. (2006). MySpace, Facebook and other social networking sites: Hot today, gone tomorrow? Retrieved September 26, 2007, from http://www.wharton.universia.net/index.cfm?fa=viewfeature&id=1156&language=english

Kolomvatsos, K. (2007). Ubiquitous computing applications in education. In M. D. Lytras & A. Naeve (Eds.), *Ubiquitous and pervasive knowledge and learning management: Semantics, social networking and new media to their full potential* (pp. 94–117). Hershey, PA: Idea Group.

Kvavik, R. B., & Caruso, J. B. (2004). ECAR study of students and information technology, 2004: Convenience, connection, and control. EDUCAUSE Center for Applied Research. Retrieved August 13, 2007, from http://www.educause.edu/LibraryDetailPage/666?Redirect=True&ID=ERS0405

Kvavik, R. B., & Caruso, J. B. (2005). ECAR study of students and information technology, 2005: Convenience, connection, and control. EDUCAUSE Center for Applied Research. Retrieved August 13, 2007, from http://educause.edu/ECAR

Laird, T. F. N., & Kuh, G. D. (2005). Student experiences with information technology and their relationship to other aspects of student engagement. *Research in Higher Education, 46*(2), 211–233.

Lampe, C., Ellison, N., & Steinfield, C. (2006, November 4–8). *A Face(book) in the crowd: Social searching vs. social browsing.* Paper presented at Computer Supported Cooperative Work, Banff, Alberta, Canada.

Lampe, C., Ellison, N., & Steinfeld, C. (2007). A familiar Face(book): Profile elements as signals in an online social network. In *Proceedings of Conference on Human Factors in Computing Systems (CHI 2007)* (pp. 435–444). New York: ACM Press.

Lanthier, R. P., & Windham, R. C. (2004). Internet use and college adjustment: The moderating role of gender. *Computers in Human Behavior, 20,* 591–606.

Lenhart, A., Madden, M., Rankin, M., & Smith, A. (2007). Teens and social media: The use of social media gains a greater foothold in teen life as they embrace the conversational nature of interactive online media. Retrieved January 2, 2008, from http://www.pewinternet.org/PPF/r/230/report_display.asp

Levy, S. (1994). *Insanely great: The life and times of Macintosh, the computer that changed everything.* New York: Viking Penguin Press.

Lewin, K. (1936). *Principles of topological psychology.* New York: McGraw-Hill.

Lewin, T. (2006). Roommates, the online version. *The New York Times.* Retrieved August 5, 2007, from http://www.nytimes.com/2006/09/13/education/13college.html?scp=1&sq=facebook+roommates&st=nyt

Li, C. (2007). Big brands and Facebook: Demographics, case studies, and best practices. Forrester Research, Inc. Retrieved December 13, 2007, from http://www.slideshare.net/charleneli/big-brands-facebook-demographics-case-studies-best-practices

Lupsa, C. (2006). A campus fad becomes a campus fact. Retrieved August 22, 2007, from http://www.csmonitor.com/2006/1213/p13s01-legn.html

Lyotard, J. (1984). *The postmodern condition: A report on knowledge.* Minneapolis, MN: University of Minnesota Press.

MacLeod, C. (2008). China vaults past USA in Internet users. Retrieved April 24, 2008, from http://www.usatoday.com/tech/world/2008-04-20-Internetusers

Malaney, G. D. (2004–2005). Student use of the internet. *Journal of Educational Technology Systems, 33*(1), 53–66.

Markham, A. N. (2005). The methods, politics, and ethics of representation in online ethnography. In N. K. Denzin & Y. S. Lincoln (Eds.), *The Sage handbook of qualitative research* (3rd ed., pp. 793–820). Thousand Oaks, CA: Sage.

Marwick, A. (2005, October). *"I'm a lot more interesting than a Friendster profile:" Identity presentation, authenticity, and power in social networking services.* Paper presented at Internet Research 6.0, Chicago.

Mashable.com (2008). United Arab Emirates block Facebook. Retrieved October 5, 2007, from http://mashable.com/2007/10/01/facebook-uae/

Matney, M., Borland, K. & Cope, M. (2008, March 10). *Facebook, blogs, and other electronic communication: How students construct new environments through social networking sites.* Paper presented at NASPA 2008 Annual Conference, Boston. Retrieved May 2, 2008, from http://www.umich.edu/~rsa

McManus, R. (2007). OpenSocial and Facebook stats from RapLeaf. Retrieved November 27, 2007, from http://www.readwriteweb.com/archives/opensocial_and_facebook_statistics.php

McMurray, J. (2008, March 29,). Colleges keeping closer watch over strange, troubled students; "Threat assessment groups" aim to prevent massacres similar to that of Virginia Tech. *The New York Times.* Retrieved April 30, 2008, from http://www.nytimes.com/articles/2008/03/29/news/nation/e2b41e642308b47f8825741a0073e829.txt

Melber, A. (2008). Facebook: The new look of surveillance. Retrieved January 30, 2008, from http://www.alternet.org/story/72556/

Meyer, K. A., & Xu, Y. J. (2007). A Bayesian analysis of the institutional and individual factors influencing faculty technology use. *Internet and Higher Education, 10,* 184–195.

Milgram, S. (1967). The small world problem. *Psychology Today, 6*(1), 62–67.

Milich, R. (2008). Michigan police bust up party promoted on Facebook. Retrieved April 10, 2008, from http://www.npr.org/templates/story/story.php?storyId=89441570

Minsky, B. D., & Marin, D. B. (1999). Why faculty members use e-mail: The role of individual differences in channel choice. *Journal of Business Communication, 36*(2), 194-211.

Morgan, G. (2003). Faculty use of course management systems. EDUCAUSE Center for Applied Research. Retrieved April 26, 2008, from http://www.educause.edu/ir/library/pdf/ers0302/rs/ers0302w.pdf

National AIDS Trust. (2007). World AIDS website launched. Retrieved March 30, 2008, from http://www.nat.org.uk/page/5858

Oblinger, D., & Oblinger, J. (2005). Educating the Net Generation: An EDUCAUSE e-book. Retrieved September 26, 2008, from http://www.educause.edu/educatingthenetgen

Palen, L. (2008, May 3). Emergency 2.0 is coming to a website near you. *New Scientist, 2654.*

Pew Internet and American Life Project. (2008). Latest trends. Retrieved May 13, 2008, from http://www.pewinternet.org/trends.asp

Powers, E. (2008). Extra eyes for athletics staff. Retrieved January 22, 2008, from http://www.insidehighered.com/news/2008/01/22/youdiligence

Press Trust of India. (2008). Facebook fast becoming dating place in Pakistan. Retrieved May 14, 2008, from http://www.ndtv.com/convergence/ndtv/story.aspx?id=NEWEN20080048814&ch=5/4/2008%204:58:00%20PM

Quinn, M., & Chmielewski, D. (2008). ITunes records a sales milestone: The digital download store overtakes Wal-Mart as the biggest U.S. music seller. *The Los Angeles Times.* Retrieved April 4, 2008, from http://www.latimes.com/technology/la-fi-itunes4apr04,1,4873885.story

Rainie, L., Kalehoff, M., & Hess, D. (2002). *College students and the web: A Pew internet data memo.* Pew Internet & American Life Project. Retrieved July 9, 2007, from http://www.pewinternet.org/

Rampell, C. (2008). Should a Facebook poster be liable for a party that became a riot? *The Chronicle of Higher Education.* Retrieved April 11, 2008, from http://chronicle.com/wiredcampus/article/2888/should-a-facebook-poster-be-liable-for-a-party-that-became-a-riot

Read, B. (2007). U. of Dayton studies professional risks of Facebook. *The Chronicle of Higher Education.* Retrieved July 9, 2007, from http://chronicle.com/weekly/v53/i19/19a03102.htm

Read, B, & Young, J. (2006, August 4). Facebook and other social-networking sites raise questions for administrators. *Chronicle of Higher Education.* Retrieved February 17, 2008, from http://chronicle.com/weekly/v52/i48/48a02901.htm.

Reed, A. (2005). Faculty and Facebook. Retrieved November 27, 2007, from http://graphic.pepperdine.edu/news/2005/2005-11-17-facultyfacebk.htm

Regan, K. (2005). Students use iTunes, even with free Napster at hand. Retrieved October 18, 2007, from http://www.ecommercetimes.com/rsstory/44531.html

Reid, R. H. (1997). *Architects of the web: 1000 days that built the future of business*. New York: Wiley.

Ricoeur, P. (2004). *On translation: Thinking in action*. London: Routledge.

Rosen, C. (2007, Summer). Virtual friendship and the new narcissism. *The New Atlantis, 17*, 15–31.

Rozwadowsk, E. (2007). Facebook and the first amendment. Retrieved August 7, 2007, from http://www.mndaily.com/articles/2007/03/21/71197

Ruhleder, K. (2000). The virtual ethnographer: Fieldwork in a distributed electronic environment. *Field Methods, 12*(3), 3–17.

Salaway, G., Katz, R. N., Caruso, J. B., Kvavik, R. B. & Nelson, M. R. (2006). The ECAR study of undergraduate students and information technology, 2006. EDUCAUSE Center for Applied Research. Retrieved January 12, 2008, from http://connect.educause.edu/Library/ECAR/Highlightsofthe2007ECARSt/45912

Salaway, G., Katz, R. N., Caruso, J. B., Kvavik, R. B., & Nelson, M. R. (2007). The ECAR study of undergraduate students and information technology, 2007. EDUCAUSE Center for Applied Research. Retrieved September 9, 2007, from http://connect.educause.edu/Library/ECAR/TheECARStudyofUndergradua/37615

Schlesinger, A. (1992). *The disuniting of America*. New York: W. W. Norton.

Schonfeld, E. (2007). Social site rankings, 2007. Retrieved December 12, 2007, from http://www.techcrunch.com/2007/11/28/social-site-rankings-october-2007/

Schwartz, J. (2007). 73 and loaded with friends on Facebook. *New York Times*. Retrieved October 16, 2007, from http://www.nytimes.com/2007/10/14/fashion/14facebook.html

Selwyn, N. (2007). The use of computer technology in university teaching and learning: A critical perspective. *Journal of Computer Assisted Learning, 23*(2), 83–94.

Sinclair, C. (1995). *NetChick: A smart-girl guide to the wired world*. New York: Henry Holt.

Slatalla, M. (2007, June 7). "omg my mom joined Facebook!!" *The New York Times*. Retrieved July, 9 2007, from http://www.nytimes.com/2007/06/07/fashion/07Cyber.html

Slater, D. (2002). Social relationships and identity online and offline. In L. A. Lievrouw & S. Livingstone (Eds.), *Handbook of new media: Social shaping and consequences of ICT* (pp. 533–546).London: Sage.

Slaughter, S., & Leslie, D. (1997). *Academic capitalism*. Baltimore, MD: Johns Hopkins University Press.

Spender, D. (1996). *Nattering on the Net: Women, power, and cyberspace*. Toronto: Garamond Press.

Stahl, B. (2004). E-teaching—The economic threat to the ethical legitimacy of education? *Journal of Information Systems Education, 15*, 155–162.

Stelter, B. (March 27, 2008). Finding political news online, the young pass it on. *The New York Times.* Retrieved April 7, 2008, from http://www.nytimes.com/2008/03/27/us/politics/27voters.html?scp=1&sq=facebook+politics+march+27+2008&st=nyt

Studentmonitor. (2008). Computing and the internet. Retrieved May 3, 2008, from http://www.studentmonitor.com/computing.php

Tapscott, D. (1998) *Growing up digital: The rise of the net generation.* New York: McGraw-Hill.

Taylor, C. (1992). *Multiculturalism and the politics of recognition: An essay.* Princeton, NJ: Princeton University Press.

Turkle, S. (1995). *Life on the screen: Identity in the age of the internet. New York: Simon & Schuster.*

UKPress.com (2008). Egyptians ignore Facebook call. Retrieved May 13, 2008, from http://ukpress.google.com/article/ALeqM5ih4wiuP_4XGhT3EJoQFblburJxIg

United Kingdom Office of Communications. (2008). Social networking: A quantitative and qualitative research report into attitudes, behaviours and uses. Retrieved April 7, 2008, from http://www.ofcom.org.uk/advice/media_literacy/medlitpub/medlitpubrss/socialnetworking/report.pdf

Valkenburg, P. M., & Schouten, P. J. (2006). Friend networking sites and their relationship to adolescents' well-being and social self-esteem. *Cyberpsychological Behavior, 9*(5), 584–590

Vander Veer, E. A. (2008). Facebook: The missing manual. Sebastopol, CA: O'Reilly Media.

Vogelstein, F. (2007, September 6). How Mark Zuckerberg turned Facebook into the web's hottest platform. Retrieved November 26, 2007, from http://www.wired.com/techbiz/startups/news/2007/09/ff_facebook

Walther, J. B., Van Der Heide, B., Kim, S-Y., Westerman, D., Tom Tong, S., & Langwell, L. (2008). The role of friends' appearance and behavior on evaluations of individuals on Facebook: Are we known by the company we keep? *Human Communication Research, 34*(1), 28–49.

Wan, Y., Kumar, V., & Bukhari, A. (2008). Will the overseas expansion of Facebook succeed? *IEEE Internet Computing, 11*(3), 69–73.

Wartman, K. L., & Savage, M. B. (2008). *Parental involvement in higher education: Understanding the relationship among students, parents, and the institution.* San Francisco: Jossey-Bass.

Web Globalization Report Card. (2008). Retrieved May 8, 2008, from http://www.bytelevel.com/.

Xu, Y. J., & Meyer, K. A. (2007). Factors explaining faculty technology use and productivity. *Internet and Higher Education, 10*(1) 41–52.

Zuckerberg, M. (2006). Statement from Mark Zuckerberg. Retrieved October 13, 2007, from http://www.nbc11.com/news/9807987/detail.html

About the Authors

Ana M. Martínez Alemán (alemanan@bc.edu) is Associate Professor of Education and Chair of the Department of Educational Administration and Higher Education at the Lynch School of Education, Boston College. Her work has appeared in the *Journal of Higher Education, the Review of Higher Education, Educational Theory, Teachers College Record,* and other scholarly journals. She has contributed to *Women in Academe: The Unfinished Agenda* (2008), *Gendered Futures in Higher Education: Critical Perspectives for Change* (2003) and *Feminist Interpretations of John Dewey* (2002). She is the coauthor (with Kristen A. Renn) of *Women in Higher Education: An Encyclopedia* (2002).

Katherine Lynk Wartman (wartmank@bc.edu) is a doctoral candidate at Boston College where her research interests include college student culture, the first-year experience, college access, and the parent–student relationship. She is also a resident director at Simmons College in Boston and has served as Parent and Family Relations and Special Projects Administrator at Colby-Sawyer College. She is the coauthor (with Marjorie B. Savage) of *Parental Involvement in Higher Education: Understanding the Relationship among Students, Parents, and the Institution* (2008), a volume in the Association for the Study of Higher Education (ASHE) Higher Education Report Series.

Index